RISE
AND
FALL
OF
GREAT EMPIRES
Spiritual Compass

**BY
SABUR ABDUL-SALAAM**

Copyright © 2024 Sabur Abdul-Salaam

All rights reserved. No part of this book may be reproduced or used in any manner without the prior written permission of the copyright owner, except for the use of brief quotations in a book review.

To request permissions, contact the publisher at:

abdulsabur319@gmail.com

Paperback: ISBN: 9798323237807

Hardcover: ISBN: 9798323238859

First hardcover edition April 2024

Cover art and layout: Khalil Abdulkhabir

DEDICATION

This book is dedicated to the Philippine people. They welcomed me and made their home my home

O mankind! We created you from a single (pair) of a male and a female, and made you into nations and tribes, that you may know each other (not that you may despise each other). Surely the most honored of you in the sight of Allah is (he who is) the most righteous of you. And Allah has full knowledge and is well acquainted (with all things).

The Quran, chapter 49, verse13

CONTENTS

DEDICATION	IV
ACKNOWLEDGMENTS	VI
PREFACE	VIII

Chapter 1
INCONSISTENCIES OF HUMAN KNOWLEDGE 1

Chapter 2
MODERN CULTURE – MUSLIM CULTURE – ISLAMIC CULTURE 7

Chapter 3
FAMILIES AND SOCIETIES 15

Chapter 4
WHEN EDUCATION IS A WEAPON OF OPPRESSION 21

Chapter 5
THE ISLAMIC RENAISSANCE 27

Chapter 6
GREED AND CULTURAL/RELIGIOUS ARROGANCE 35

Chapter 7
CAUSE AND EFFECT 43

Chapter 8
CULTURE/SOCIAL NORMS 49

Chapter 9
A FIFTY-YEAR JOURNEY TO FIND OUT WHY? 55

Chapter 10
DIGNITY OF WORK 63

Chapter 11
CRIME AND CRIMINOLOGY 69

Chapter 12
DIVINE, NATURAL AND HUMAN POWER 75

EPILOGUE 85
BIBLIOGRAPHY 89

ACKNOWLEDGMENTS

It is only fitting that I begin the acknowledgments of this book by saying Al Hamdullilah, all praise is due to Allah, for any part of this book that may be praise worthy. Secondly, I have to acknowledge Safaa Alshiraida, my spiritual mentor for the past 45 years, and my sahabah Khalil Abdulkhabir, who has always been a source of both inspiration and technical assistance. They both were very helpful during the early stages of volume two. I also have to mention Dr. Bilal Philips (The clash of Civilizations [an Islamic view]). He is truly a scholar of both Islamic and Western culture. Next I have to mention Shaykh Sayyid Abul A'la Mawdudi (Toward Understanding the Quran), and Shaykh Abdullah Yusuf Ali (The Holy Quran), and Shaykh Muhammad Al-Ghazali (A Thematic Commentary on the Quran), may Allah reward them for their contribution to enabling English speaking Muslims (including myself) to have a better understanding of the Quran. Next I need to acknowledge Shaykh Yusuf al Qaradawi (The Lawful and the Prohibited In Islam), this book in particular provided an invaluable service to the 20th and 21st centuries' common Muslims, helping us to distinguish between the halal and the haram. Sayyed Abul Hasan Ali Nadwi (Islam and the World) also needs to be added to this list of illustrious scholars for producing a book to help the common Muslim know how the Muslim Ummah went from being a superpower to where we are now. May all the Muslims that I have mentioned, one day have a home in Paradise.

I also want to thank Rachel Maligas who was very helpful with the preparation of the final draft, and Openstax (Introduction to Sociology), the publishing company of Rice University. I am also appreciative of Jeffrey Sachs (The Ages of Globalization) for helping me to see globalization from a historical perspective. And equally powerful but much more painful was Marc Lamont Hill's book, NOBODY! The painful but important lesson that I learned from his book was that the Declaration of Independence may be the most hypocritical document in existence.

The writing of volume two was a real learning experience for me but before concluding my list of acknowledgments, there are still a few individuals that need to be mentioned: Shaykh Mahmoud Esma'il Sieny (Heroes of Islam) needs to be mentioned because of his contribution to chapter five. It is also imperative that I mention Dr. Abdullah Hakim Quick (The Forty Ahaadeeth on Islamic Revival) because without his contribution my epilogue would have been incomplete. May Allah bless and have mercy on everyone who has contributed to Volume two becoming a reality, both those who are living as well as those who have already passed away. This includes both those I have mentioned by name and the countless number of contributors who I have not mentioned by name. However, there is still one person left that needs to be mentioned because of the life changing lessons that I have learned from him. I am referring to Shaykh Sayyid Qutb (Milestones), who exemplified what it means to be a true follower of the Prophet Muhammad (Peace and blessings of Allah be upon him).

PREFACE

According to science, something cannot come from nothing which means that something has always existed. But there is a major disagreement as to what that something was. You have the "Creation Theory" and the "Big Bang theory." The Creation Theory (a religious theory) that states our Creator always existed and that He created the universe and everything in it. However, the Big Bang Theory (a secular theory) is how astronomers explain the way the universe began. It is the idea that the universe began as just a single point, then expanded and stretched to grow as large as it is right now - and it is still stretching!

> **Charles Darwin's Theory of Evolution attempted to explain human existence in terms of natural forces and not a supernatural creator. "In his book, The Origin of the species, Darwin implied that humans shared their origins with the ape which, like all other forms of multicellular life, evolved from unicellular organisms through a process which he named 'natural selection' but which became commonly known as 'survival of the fittest'."[1]**

Two theories (the Creation Theory and the Big Bang Theory), yet it is permissible to teach one in American public schools but the other one is not. Why is that the case when we don't have what is normally considered "empirical proof" for either? The reason is secularism has won its war against religion.

> **"Secularism is a system of beliefs which rejects all forms of religious faith and worship. It is also the view that public education and other matters of civil policy should be conducted without the introduction of a religious element. In the medieval period, there was a strong tendency for religious persons to despise human affairs and to meditate on God and the afterlife. As a reaction to this medieval tendency, secularism, at the time of the Renaissance, exhibited itself in the development of humanism, when man began to show more interest in human**

cultural achievements and the possibilities of his fulfillment in this world. The movement toward secularism has been in progress during the entire course of modern history."[2]

The roots of western culture (and education) can be placed back to the Greco-Roman civilizations. Greece and Rome were relatively civilized while the rest of Europe existed in a state of savagery. But what they had in common with the rest of Europe was they worshiped many gods. And when you study their mythology, you will find the gods were worshiped as idols in human form.[3]

In their mythology you will also find that there were often conflicts between the gods and the humans and usually it was the humans who outsmarted the gods. So it stands to reason that education that has a Greco-Roman foundation, would come to the conclusion that human beings are the superior intellect in existence.

So in volume two, I am going to be discussing people and life in general, both past and present, from both secular and religious points of view. The secular points of view will usually come from a historical or sociological source, while the religious point of view will usually be based on the religion of Islam. I have chosen the religion of Islam for two reasons: It is a way of life with laws governing all areas of life (even though the same can be said for Orthodox Judaism) and my second reason is I am a retired Muslim chaplain and have spent many years studying the religion of Islam.

In volume one I described America's rise and some of the reasons for its decline. I also pointed out that the truth can sometimes be a bitter pill, but it is a pill that must be taken if we want our sick society to become healthy again. So the solution to America's problems, and the rest of mankind's problems, can only be found by going back to square one, the cause of the problem.

ENDNOTES

[1] Philips, Abu Ameenah Bilal, The Clash of Civilizations (An Islamic View) Pages 20 & 21, Al-Hidayah Publishing and Distribution LTD, 2007
[2] Ibid, Page 22
[3] Ibid, Page 14

Chapter 1

INCONSISTENCIES OF HUMAN KNOWLEDGE

Did the unbelievers not realize that the heavens and the earth was one solid mass, then we tore them apart, and we made every living being out of water? Will they then not believe? [1]

Religious beliefs preceded secularism and yet since the Renaissance, secularism has almost completely replaced any influence of religion in both public education and civil policy in most of the modern "developed" nations of the world. To try to understand how this came about, it is important that we look at the history and philosophical foundation of western culture/education. Since the roots of western culture can be traced back to the Greco-Roman civilizations, it would make sense to begin by looking at Greek culture.

If one wants to begin to understand the intellectual, ethical and aspirational evolution of the western mind he/she would have to begin with the Greek civilization. The following four points summarize the intellectual fundamentals of the Ancient Greeks.

1. Disregard of transcendental truths
2. Want of religious feeling and spirituality
3. Worship of material comfort
4. Exaggerated patriotism

Greek civilization was purely materialistic. The Greeks could not even conceive of God without giving Him physical forms and shapes, and making images for His Attributes and installing them in their temples so as to lend a visible aspect to their devotion. They had a god of sustenance, a god of benevolence, a god of fury, and so on. [2]

The following quote is an excerpt taken from a lecture on European civilization given by Dr. Haas a German scholar, given in Geneva.

> **"What is European civilization?"** He held that the first stage for European civilization was set by Ancient Greece where: "the aim was to develop man harmoniously. The supreme measure was a beautiful body. It clearly emphasized the senses. Physical education - games and dancing - and mental education - poetry, music, drama, philosophy, even the sciences - were kept in proportion so as to develop the mind but not at the expense of the body. Its religion had no spirituality, no theology, no mysticism.[3]
>
> The best way to describe the Ancient Greeks' religiosity would be to call them agnostics. The Greeks did not deny the existence of God, they just assumed that God did not play an important part in their life. Their assumption was God created them and their intellect but then retreated into seclusion.[4]

Another major point that needs to be mentioned is western nationalism. Initially European nationalism was uniquely different from nationalism in other parts of the world and that may have had to do with geographical reasons. In some regions the climate and vast amount of fertile land made it very easy to support human life. But Europe was divided by natural barriers like mountains and deep rivers, consequently, dividing its population into many territorial units. So the population in some areas were very dense, making the means of subsistence scarce. This added to Western Nationalism/Patriotism.

> The entire civilization of the Greeks was built around their city-states. Lecky says that the state occupied a predominance in the Greek mind and virtue was firmly connected with patriotism. The cosmopolitanism of Socrates and Anaxagoras had made little impression upon the Hellenes. Aristotle's system of ethics was based on differentiation between the Greeks and non-Greeks. According to him, the Greeks had no more obligations to barbarians (foreigners) than to wild beasts.[5]

Now let us look at Roman Civilization. When the Romans' only priority was their military, the Greek civilization already had outstanding achievements in the areas of literature and philosophy. So when Romans conquered the Greeks they saw no reason to reinvent the wheel, they just borrowed from the Greeks' intellectual achievements and manners.

It is also evident that the Greeks, having had for several centuries a splendid literature, at a time when the Romans had none, and when the Latin language was still too crude for literary purposes, the period in which the Romans first emerged from a purely military condition would bring with it an ascendancy of Greek ideas. Fabius Pictor and Cincius Alimentus, the earliest native historians, both wrote in Greek.[6]

Initially, the one thing the two great civilizations had in common was their worship of pagan gods. As the Romans advanced culturally, they too decided that the gods play no part in the management of worldly affairs. Religion in Ancient Rome was just a social tradition, a selfish method of obtaining prosperity, averting calamities and reading the future. "Ancient Rome produced many heroes, but no saints. Its self sacrifices were patriotic not religious. Its' religion was neither an independent teacher nor a source of inspiration."[7]

However, religion in the Roman empire went through a revolutionary change in 305 C.E. (Christian Era) when Constantine ascended to the throne because Christianity became the official religion of the Roman Empire. Constantine's victory was the result of his Christian supporters' heroic sacrifices which earned them a generous share in the affairs of Constantine's empire. But some say Christianity gained an empire but lost its soul.

Place, power, profit - these were in view of whoever now joined the conquering sect. Crowds of worldly persons, who cared nothing about its religious ideas, became its warmest supporters. Pagans at heart, their influence was soon manifested in the paganization of Christianity that ensued forthwith.

Though the Christian party had proved itself sufficiently strong to give a master to the Empire, it was never sufficiently strong to destroy its antagonist, paganism. The issue of struggle between them was an amalgamation of the principles of both. In this, Christianity differed from Mohammedanism which absolutely annihilated its antagonist and spread its own doctrines without adulteration.[8]

THE STRUGGLE BETWEEN RELIGION AND SCIENCE

Europe's Dark Ages was the Golden Age of Islam. The age when the Muslim world experienced their intellectual renaissance (more details will be given in a later chapter), which later inspired Europes' renaissance. European thinkers and scientists broke their chains of intellectual slavery. Religious theories that were based on **preposterous evidence** were boldly refuted using scientific methods.

> The great transition to modern science occurred in the battle over Copernicus's theory - the Copernican revolution. Galileo was the hero of this battle. He claimed that the observations of the heavens he had made with his new telescope vindicated Copernicus's theory: Contrary to what people had thought for centuries, the sun was fixed and the earth orbited around it and rotated on an axis. This novel idea was annoying to the followers of Aristotle who conspired against him to get the church to silence him and ultimately convict him as a heretic.[9]

The churches' ruthless response was the inquisition. No "heretic" in houses, towns, countryside or caves were safe. "It is estimated that between 1481 and 1801, the Inquisition punished three hundred and forty thousand people, nearly two thousand of whom were burnt alive."

> Galileo committed the very serious sin of believing that the sun was not at a fixed place in the sky. He was imprisoned and punished until he died. Provoked by the clergy's intellectual stagnation and the atrocities of the Inquisition, the educated segment of the European population began rejecting all knowledge, morality and truth related to the church and religion in general. The struggle between Christianity and secular knowledge eventually took the form of a struggle between religion and progress or in other words, religion is incompatible with science.[10]

> So on the one hand, and rightly so, the church was wrong for not supporting the Copernican Theory, but it is okay for science to say that human origins began between 7,000,000 and 2,000,000 B.C. and on the same page say, "The first written records of human activity date from about 5,500 years ago; anything that happened before that time is known as prehistoric. We know about this distant era only through archaeological excavations and ancient settlements and the painstaking work of anthropologists examining ancient bones and fossils." And it is also okay to say that humans and apes evolved from a common ancestor that lived between ten and five million years ago which scientists refer to as hominids. Lucy is the name given to 40% of a

hominid fossil skull that was discovered in Ethiopia and it is one of the most complete hominid fossil skulls that has been discovered. Lucy's partial skull is supposed to be empirical proof that man has evolved from an ape.[11]

The following is a quote from Shaykh Muhammad Al-Ghazali, a 20th Century Islamic Scholar, giving what he considers to be his reasonable Islamic explanation:

> The Qur'an does not say anything about the human generations that lived before Noah. This leads me to suspect the accuracy of archaeological and geological findings of a human skull (human skull not hominid) tens of millions of years old.[12]

ENDNOTES

[1] Mawdudi, Sayyid Abul A'la, Toward Understanding the Quran, Page 677, The Islamic Foundation, 2006
[2] Nadwi, Sayyed Abul Hasan Ali, Islam and the World, Page 103, UK Islamic Academy, 2005
[3] Ibid, Page 103
[4] Ibid, Page 104
[5] Ibid, Page 106
[6] Ibid, Page 106
[7] Ibid, Page 107
[8] Ibid, Pages 109 & 110
[9] Philips, Bilal, Clash of Civilizations (An Islamic View), Page 18, Al-Hidaayah Publishing and Distribution, 2007
[10] Nadwi, Sayyed Abbul Hasan Ali, Islam and the World, Pages 117 & 118, UK Islamic Academy, 2005
[11] Wolf, Alex, A Short History of the World, Page 8, Metro Books, 2008
[12] Al-Ghazali, Muhammad, A Thematic Commentary on the Qur'an, Page 151, The International Institute of Islamic Thought, 2000

Chapter 2

MODERN CULTURE – MUSLIM CULTURE – ISLAMIC CULTURE

Fair in the eyes of men is the love of things they Covet: women and sons; heaped-up hoards of Gold and silver; horses branded (for blood and excellence); and (wealth of) cattle and well-tilled Land. Such are the possessions of this world's Life; but in nearness to Allah is the best of goals.[1]

MODERN WESTERN CULTURE

It was Charles Lyell's book Principles of Geology, published in 1830, that helped usher in Modern Western Culture. Prior to then the majority of the people, including the intellectual elites, were religious believers.

> Until the 19th century, the vast majority of people and even a significant portion of the intellectual elite remained religious believers. Then came the final blow: the coming of age of the two "historical" sciences, geology and biology. In the early 19th century, many scientists still thought the Old Testament gave the literal account of the early history of the world, and they came up with a history of the earth based on the first books of the Bible. They computed the age of the earth from the biblical genealogies. They explained the irregularities of the earth with reference to Noah's flood. The theory was known as catastrophism and its proponents saw it as a way of vindicating belief in God with reference to nature.[2]

In general, "culture" is considered shared religious beliefs, values and practices, but after the 19th century, religion played a much less significant role concerning people's beliefs and values. People being social creatures, we have always grouped together in small communities to survive. Living together we had common habits and behaviors and this is all part of a community's culture. But sociologists define a "community" as a definable region as small as a neighborhood or as large as a country. So people who share a community and culture are usually referred to as a "society", and the words culture and society are sometimes used interchangeably. Human behaviors are learned behaviors and religions were a very important source of peoples' learned behaviors prior to the 19th century. Families are a very important part of a community, but before the 20th century, a family usually consisted of a husband, wife, children and grandparents which is in accordance with most religious teachings' but after the 20th century the definition of family changes drastically in Western Societies.[3]

MUSLIM CULTURE

The Quranic expression "Deen al-Islam" is usually translated as "the religion of Islam", but a better translation is "the Islamic way of life", because in the West religion consists of spiritual beliefs and religious acts (prayer, fasting, charity, etc.). However, in the Quran, Allah's last divine revelation, and the authentic traditions of the Prophet Muhammad ibn Abdullah, there is divine and prophetic guidance concerning all areas of life, so any lawful action a Muslim does in accordance with Islamic guidance are acts of worship.

However, Cultural Islam or Folk Islam as Christian missionaries refer to it, Islamic practices have become mixed with local customs and traditions, generally handed down from earlier generations. "Some cultural practices are based on authentic Islamic traditions, while many are not. However, the cultural Muslim is unable to distinguish between the two."[4] The following are cultural Islam's four sources of un-Islamic traditions: Pre-Islamic practices, adopted practices, religious innovations and factionalism.

1. Pre-Islamic Practices

When Islam spread to various parts of the world, people who

embraced the faith brought into Islam some of their pre-Islamic traditions. Islamic law did not prohibit all the practices of the people whom it governed. A special category of laws called URF made allowances for local customs. Consequently, local traditions were permitted as long as they did not contradict clear commandments in the religion. The amount of un-Islamic customs which were carried into Islam by new converts depended on the degree to which they learned Islam and the knowledge of those who invited them to Islam. The more ignorant of Islamic teachings, the easier it was for them to continue their pre-Islamic habits. Likewise, those who taught the new converts, would tolerate un-Islamic habits which they were ignorant of. For example, the red wedding dress of most Pakistani and Indian Muslims is identical to the Hindu wedding dress. There is no specified color for the wedding dress according to Islamic law. It can be any color, as long as it is not an imitation of the religious ceremonies of other religions. Consequently, white commonly used by Christians and red by Hindus should not be used.[5]

The wearing of a white or red wedding dress may seem harmless but other inherited practices may be both physically and spiritually harmful and a cultural Muslim may do them thinking they are doing something that Islam requires them to do. "For example, the Pharaonic circumcision of females (genital mutilation) as practiced in East Africa, the Sudan and Egypt among Muslims and non-Muslims tribes of that region is another example of inherited un-Islamic practices."[6]

2. Adopted Practices

It is not unusual for groups of people to adopt practices of other groups especially when those practices are very popular or well known. For example, 400 years after the death of the Prophet Muhammad (PBUH) the Muslims in Egypt began celebrating the Prophet's birthday because they were imitating the Christian's celebration of Christmas. Another example is the practice of building tombs over graves. This practice was the motivation for the building of the Taj Mahal.

Mughal emperor Shah Jahan had it built in the memory of his wife Mumtaz Mahal in the year 1649. It cost 40 million rupees to build, money that could have been used to help the millions of poor people in India, and in other cases it caused the evil practice of making some graves into places of worship.

Shrines can be found all over the Muslim world and the masses of ignorant Muslims flock to them to perform worship in their vicinity and to ask favors of the dead. A classical example is that of the shrine of Shaykh Mu'in ud-Din Chisti (d. 1236), in Ajmer, Rajasthan state, northwest India. This shrine is the center of pilgrimage for Muslims in the Indian subcontinent.[7]

The Fifth Pillar of Islam is to make the pilgrimage to Mecca not India.

3. Religious Innovation

One of the main causes of religious innovation is the belief of "mysticism." Mysticism is defined as an experience of union with God and the belief that man's main goal lies in seeking that union." One of the origins of the mysticism concept were the Greek philosophers. In Plato's Symposium, he describes how there is a ladder of ascent by which man through his consistent and sincere effort his soul could eventually attain union with God. There is also a parallel concept in Hinduism where the human soul (the Atman) can achieve the Realization of the Brahman (the impersonal absolute) which is the ultimate goal of existence and will no longer have to be Reborn again.

The Mystic tradition kept alive in monastic Christianity began to find expression among Muslims from about 8th century CE, a century after the borders of the Islamic state had expanded to include Egypt and Syria and its major centers of monasticism. A group of Muslims who were not satisfied with what the Shari'ah (IslamicLaw) had to offer, developed a parallel system which they named the Tariqah (the way). Just as the ultimate goal of the Hindu was unity with the world soul and the Christian mystic union with God; the ultimate goal of this movement became Fana, the dissolution of the ego, and Wusul, the meeting and unification of the human soul with Allah in this life.[8]

4. Religious Factionalism and Fanaticism in General

The religion of Islam does not just consist of religious rituals, it is a total way of life. So Islamic laws can be put into five general categories: obligatory acts (fard), recommended acts (mandub), permissible acts but not recommended (mubah), discouraged acts (makruh) and forbidden acts (haram). Muslims who want to have an in-depth understanding of Islamic laws, it is necessary for him or her to study both the Shari'ah and Fiqh.

> Islamically, Shari'ah refers to the sum total of Islamic laws which was revealed to the Prophet Muhammad (pbuh) and recorded in the Qur'an as well as deducible from the Prophet's divinely guided lifestyle called the sunnah.
>
> Fiqh literally means, the true understanding of what is intended. An example of this usage can be found in the Prophet Muhammad's statement: "To whomsoever Allah wishes good, He gives the Fiqh (true understanding) of the religion." Technically, however, Fiqh refers to 'the science of deducing Islamic laws from evidence found in the sources of Islamic laws'. The main tool of Fiqh is Ijtihad (reasoned ruling) which operates through Ijma (consensus) and Qiyas (deduction by analogy). By extension, the term Fiqh has also come to mean... Madh-hab, the body of deduced Islamic laws.[9]

Many of the close companions of the Prophet Muhammad were the first scholars of Islam. In their effort to spread the religion they traveled to different parts of the world and would have students who they taught the religion too. Their schools of thought became known as Madhahabs. In the early days there were many Madhahabs but eventually it dwindled down to four (three major and one minor). These schools of thought took on such an important part of many Muslims' lives, the practice began of Muslims naming themselves after their respective Madhahab. Then after the sacking of Baghdad in 1258 (C.E.) and the execution of the last (Arab) caliph, Al-Muta'sim, the door to Ijtihad (reasoned ruling) was closed which opened the door to taqlid (blind following of aMadh-hab).

> Scholars of this period left all forms of Ijtihad and unanimously issued a legal ruling which was intended to close the door of Ijtihad permanently. They reasoned that all possible issues had already been raised and addressed, and there was therefore no need for further Ijtihad.[10]

One could also say that taqlid opened the door to religious fanaticism. It was just a question of going from blindly following a school of thought, to blindly following a Muslim leader.

> The topic of Muslim culture would not be complete without including what I call "Modern Muslim Culture." It is not just a

practice of "adopting practices," It is the total acceptance of a new criterion for determining what is right or wrong. The vision of modern Muslim culture has been blinded by the glamor of Western civilization. Western civilization for some Muslims, has become their object of worship. They humbly accept Western principles and customs unquestionably without a doubt. Those Western principles and customs that agree with Islam, they praise them. But those that oppose Islam, they make excuses and apologies, surrendering to the philosophy and customs of Western civilization. They permit things which Islam has prohibited such as statues, lotteries and the paying of interest. And they find distasteful things which Islam has permitted like divorce and polygamy. In other words, what is legal in the West is halal (lawful) and whatever is illegal is haram (unlawful).[11]

ISLAMIC CULTURE

Islamic Culture represents the traditions and customs which evolve from the day-to-day practice of people following the authentic teachings of Islam. In general, when the various cultures of Muslims around the world are compared, the common features found in all countries and regions represent the core Islamic culture, and the variations represent the basic features of Muslim culture.

For example, the dress of Muslim women varies in color, style and material according to Muslim culture. However, they all share the basic Islamic cultural principle of covering the whole body except for or including face and hands.[12]

Islamic Culture is based on Islamic beliefs and practices, and the foundation of these beliefs and practices are the six pillars of eman (faith) and the five pillars of Islam (acknowledging the One God and the Prophet Muhammad ibn Abdullah, the five daily prayers, fasting the month of Ramadan, paying the annual zakat (charity) and making the pilgrimage to Mecca at least once. These beliefs and practices are supposed to produce morality, the quality of conforming to the principles of good conduct.

Islamic Morality - "The Islamic system of morality is a complete system that governs human relations with God, with other humans and with the environment." Islamic morality is very different from Democratic morality. "In the democratic

system, moral values are set according to the preference of the majority."[13]

One of the reasons the Egyptian military was able to regain power after the "Arab Spring" revolution was because the new democratically elected government tried to establish a government based on Islam but the majority of the demonstrators who participated in the revolution wanted a Western style "liberal democracy."

ENDNOTES

[1] Ali, Abdullah Yusuf, The Holy Quran, Page 32, Goodword Books, 2007
[2] Philips, Abu Ameenah Bilal, The Clash of Civilizations (An Islamic View), Page 19, Al Hidaayah Publishing and Distribution LTD, 2007
[3] Openstax, Introduction to Sociology 2E, Page 53, Rice University, 2016
[4] Philips, Abu Ameenah Bilal, The Clash of Civilizations (An Islamic View), Page 3, Al Hidaayah Publishing and Distribution LTD, 2007
[5] Ibid. Page 35
[6] Ibid. Page 35
[7] Ibid. Pages 38-39
[8] Ibid. Pages 40-41
[9] Ibid. Page 44
[10] Ibid. Page 48
[11] Qaradawi, Yusuf al, The Lawful and Prohibited In Islam, Pages 2-3, Dar Al Taqwa LTD, 2007
[12] Philips, Abu Ameenah Bilal, The Clash of Civilizations (An Islamic View), Page 63, Al Hidaayah Publishing and Distribution LTD, 2007
[13] Ibid. Page 67

Chapter 3

FAMILIES AND SOCIETIES

It is He Who has created man from water: then He has established relationships of lineage and Marriage: for your Lord has power (over all things). [1]

Allah created Adam and then created his spouse producing the first human family and all the societies of the world sprang from that first family. Allah created human beings to worship Him and establish His way of life on earth in exchange for eternity in Paradise.

Surely Allah has purchased of the believers their lives and their belongings and in return has promised that they shall have Paradise. [2]

But those disbelievers who worship wealth and power had to produce an alternative story (the big bang theory) because true religion does not permit people to kill and exploit one another in pursuit of money, so religious beliefs and practices had to be corrupted and the first step was to replace the worship of the Creator with the worship of many gods. One of the methods that was used to bring this about was the concept of divide and conquer, and one of its earliest forms was tribalism which eventually evolved into nationalism. The leaders of the disbelievers were able to erase from the memory of many people that they were all part of the human family, then at other times in history, racism became the main form of divide and conquer. Another method that was used was the replacing of divine knowledge with human information. So eventually the secularization of culture was established in modern societies.

Sociologists are interested in the relationship between the institution of marriage and the institution of family because,

historically, marriages are what creates a family, and families are the most basic social unit upon which society is built...So what is a family? A husband, a wife, and two children–maybe even a pet–has served as the model for the traditional U.S. family for most of the twentieth century.[3]

However, in the 21st century the concepts of marriage and the family became much more complex. Now sociologists ask what is marriage? Different people now define marriage in different ways.

Not even sociologists are able to agree on a single meaning. For our purposes, we'll define "marriage" as a legally recognized social contract between two people, traditionally based on a sexual relationship and implying a permanence of the union. In practicing cultural relativism, we should also consider variations, such as whether a legal union is required (think of "common law" marriage and its equivalents), or whether more than two people can be involved (consider polygamy). Other variations on the definition of marriage might include whether spouses are of opposite sexes or the same sex and how one of the traditional expectations of marriage (to produce children) is understood today.[4]

So the 21st century family model differs from the 20th century family model in that it now includes single parent households, as well as a homosexual couple without children. A primary area of debate for sociologists is exactly what constitutes a family? This is also an important area of debate for politicians and some religious leaders.

Family structure is very important for social conservatives, with family members filling certain roles: father, mother, children etc. But sociologists usually use a different yardstick, defining family members based on the way they relate to each other. A sociologist may define a family "as a socially recognized group (usually joined by blood, marriage, cohabitation, or adoption)) that forms an emotional connection and serves as an economic unit of society."[5]

A religious person may wonder why it was necessary for science to replace religion in most modern societies. However, the answer has already been given in the previously mentioned verse of the Quran. "Surely Allah has purchased of the believers their lives and their belongings and in return has promised that they shall have paradise." Sayyid Mawdudi's commentary on the verse says the following:

When a man has true faith it involves a commitment to devote himself sincerely to God and thus attain His reward in return for the commitment. This two way commitment has been described as a "transaction". What this means is that faith is in fact a contract according to which man places all that he has – his life, his wealth – at the disposal of God; he "sells" them to God. In return, he accepts God's promise of Paradise in the next life.[6]

It is obvious that the 1% would prefer the type of people who are willing to eat, drink and be merry knowing that tomorrow they may die, as opposed to those who are willing to live modest lives, willing to make sacrifices for their families or their communities' in the hope of being rewarded in the Hereafter. Societies consist of communities and communities consist of families so if you want to secularize a society, you begin with the family. The Quran says:

> **It is He who created you from a single person, and made his mate of a like nature, in order that he might dwell with her (in love). When they are united, she bears a light burden and carries it about (unnoticed). When she grows heavy, they both pray to Allah their Lord, (saying): "If you give us a goodly child, we vow we shall (ever) be grateful.**[7]

That is very different from "a socially recognized group (usually joined by blood, marriage, cohabitation, or adoption) that forms an emotional connection and serves as an economic unit of society". It is true that religion provides people with moral and ethical ideals but a family should not be reduced to just an economic unit of society. There was a time when parents made sacrifices to save for their children's college education so after graduation their children could get jobs and use their savings to buy a house instead of having to pay off student loans.

> In the latter part of the twentieth century, American life [for some people] changed drastically. A man could no longer follow his father and grandfather into a good paying manufacturing job or join a union that guaranteed jobs with good wages and benefits. With the introduction of the birth control pill in the 1960s, it became easier to have intimate relationships [not

having to fear pregnancy] without marriage. And many people no longer had confidence in the traditional religions.[8]

How could this have happened in the United States, people not being able to find good paying jobs with good benefits, in a country that had a governing philosophy (in theory) "of the people, by the people and for the people". Some people might place the blame on globalization and government policies like the North American Free Trade Agreement (NAFTA). Canada, the United States and Mexico agreed to much freer trade opportunities that excluded normal tariffs and import laws, making it easier to conduct international trade. Politicians and economists presented all the possible trade opportunities but neglected to mention the possible problems like decreases in job opportunities. Once jobs could be outsourced to workers in Mexico, American workers became less competitive and had to settle for lower paying jobs with less job security. For decades, the white American middle-class had no problem with racism preventing minorities from being competitive.

WHAT GOES AROUND COMES AROUND[9]

The governing philosophy of the United States was in theory, "of the people, by the people and for the people." But the reality has always been for the government to serve the interest of the rich. "Not that the rich agreed among themselves; they had disputes over policies. But the purpose of the state was to settle upper-class disputes peacefully, control lower-class rebellion, and adopt policies that would further the long range stability of the system." Rutherford Hayes' election in 1877 set the tone. It didn't matter if a Democrat or Republican won the election because in either case, national policies and priorities would basically remain the same.[10]

The 1% controls economic policies but not necessarily social norms. Considering the fact that there was a time when the majority of Americans believed in God and the marriage institution should be restricted to the union of a male and a female, how did we arrive at the point where two men or two women can now be legally married in the United States? Framing/frame Analysis may be the answer to that question. During the second half of the 20th century sociologists developed the concept of "Frames" to explain how individuals identify and understand social events and which norms they should follow in any given situation.[11]

Successful social movements use three kinds of frames (Snow and Bedford 1988) to further their goals. The first type, diagnostic framing, states the problem in a clear, easily understood way. When applying diagnostic frames, there are no shades of gray: instead, there is the belief that what "they " do is wrong and this is how "we" will fix it. The anti-gay marriage movement is an example of diagnostic framing with its uncompromising insistence that marriage is only between a man and a woman. [Where were the Muslims?] Prognostic framing, the second type, offers a solution and states how it will be implemented. Some examples of this frame, when looking at the issue of marriage equality as framed by the anti-gay marriage movement, include the plan to restrict marriage to "one man/one woman" or to allow only "civil unions" instead of marriages. As you can see, there may be many competing prognostic frames even within social movements adhering to similar diagnostic frames. Finally, motivational framing is the call to action: what should you do once you agree with the diagnostic frame and believe in the prognostic frame? These frames are action oriented. In the gay marriage movement, a call to action might encourage you to vote "no" on Proposition 8 in California (a move to limit marriage to male-female couples), or conversely, to contact your local congressperson to express your viewpoint that marriage should be restricted to male-female couples.[12]

The economic suffering of the middle-class caused by the deindustrialization of the 1970s created a crisis forcing the ruling elites to devise a new political paradigm. They did not want the middle-class to know that they were suffering as a result of corporate greed, so they shifted the blame to the New Deal welfare state that was started by Franklin D. Roosevelt, and was now supporting criminal black youth, welfare queens and other social parasites. This opened the door to Ronald Reagan's authoritarian populism. Reagan also (rhetorically) "championed family values, traditional morality, individual autonomy, law and order, the Christian faith, and a return to a mythical past, at least for white Americans."[13]

ENDNOTES

[1] Ali, Abdullah Yusuf. The Holy Quran, Page 252, Goodword Books, 2007
[2] Maududi, Sayyid Abul A'la, Toward Understanding the Quran, Page 411, The Islamic Foundation, 2006
[3] Openstax, Introduction to Sociology 2E, Page 309, Rice University, 2016
[4] Ibid. Page 309
[5] Ibid. Page 309
[6] Maududi, Sayyid Abul A'la, Toward Understanding the Quran, Page 411, The Islamic Foundation, 2006
[7] Ali, Abdullah Yusuf, The Holy Quran, Page 114, Goodword Books, 2007
[8] Abdul-Salaam, Sabur, Rise and Fall of Great Empires – Black Lives Matter, Page 100, Sabur Abdul-Salaam, 2021
[9] Ibid. Pages 99 & 100
[10] Ibid. Page 62
[11] Openstax, Introduction to Sociology 2E, Page 484, Rice University, 2016
[12] Ibid. Page 484
[13] Hedges, Chris, America: The Farewell Tour, Page 5, Simon and Schuster, 2018

Chapter 4

WHEN EDUCATION IS A WEAPON OF OPPRESSION

> **Read! And your Lord is the Most Generous. Who Taught by the pen – taught humanity what they knew not. Most certainly, one exceeds all bounds Once they think they are self-sufficient. But surely To your Lord is the return of all.** [1]

One may wonder why Americans have tolerated poverty/income inequality, racism, gender inequality and environmental abuse for so long, and why millions of poor and middle-class Trump followers have continued to support him even after it became obvious that the vast majority of his policies favored the wealthy. Part of the blame has to be placed on the American public school system.

> Even though the systems may be very different, every nation in the world has an educational institution through which a society's children are taught basic academic knowledge, learning skills, and cultural norms. [2]

IDEOLOGY AND SCHOOL CURRICULUM

In a book entitled Ideology and Curriculum, Michael Apple (1979) discusses the relationship between the curriculum content of schools and the ideological orientation of the society in which the school is embedded. He traces the history of the curriculum orientation of American public schools to a conservative ideology whose primary objective was the maintenance of social control and the elimination of cultural differences within the American people. According to Apple, "any serious attempt to understand whose knowledge gets into schools must be, by its very nature, historical. It must begin by seeing current arguments about curriculum, pedagogy, and institutional control as outgrowth of specific historical conditions, as arguments that were and are generated by the roles schools have played in our social order."(p.65) Apple notes that the early developers of school curricula saw a need to differentiate between the kind of education received by those who would rule society and those who would be ruled. "This view of the unequal distribution of responsibility and power was reflected when they talked about how curriculum differentiation would fulfill two social purposes: education for the leadership and education for what they called 'followership". Those of high intelligence were to be educated to lead the nation by being taught to understand the needs of society. They would also learn to define appropriate beliefs and standards of behavior to meet those needs. The mass of the population were to be taught to accept these beliefs and standards whether or not they understand them or agreed with them."(p.75) "Those of high intelligence" obviously referred to Caucasian men with money, while the "mass of the population" was everyone else.[3]

When looking at American public schools, one would think that the states that have the highest graduation rates would also be the states that have the fewest students per teacher, and the teachers received the highest salaries and had the highest expenditure per student. But surprisingly, that is not what the statistical information for the school year 2016-2017 showed. New Jersey was number two with a graduation rate of 90.5% while having 11.8 pupils per teacher, and their average teacher's salary was $69,917 and a $20,171 expenditure per pupil. Washington D.C. was number 50 with a graduation rate of 73.2%, while having a 12.7 pupil per teacher and their average teacher's salary was $76,486 and a $21,001 expenditure per pupil. Considering the fact that there are probably a considerable number of students who are the children of government officials in the Washington D.C. public schools, it would be interesting to see what the school budgets were in Washington D.C. majority and minority school districts.[4]

For those who wonder how American students compare with students from other countries in mathematics [the language of science], tests that were given in 2000 and 2015 that were graded on a scale of 0 to 1000, in the year 2000 American students scored

493 which was number 20 of 31 countries and in 2015 American students scored 470, number 42 of 70 countries.[5]

American students' results are less than praise worthy considering the United States is the richest country in the world. But what early American educators may have failed to realize was that when you lower the educational possibilities for the masses, you are automatically lowering the competitiveness of the elites because it becomes easier to be outstanding.

EDUCATION, TECHNOLOGY AND THE 21ST CENTURY

As always with American history in general and American public school education in particular, there has always been a double standard. And this has also proven to be true in the areas of education and technology. "Since the beginning of the millennium, social science researchers have tried to bring attention to the digital divide, the uneven access to technology among the different races, classes and geographic areas."[6]

There are two forms of technological stratification. The first is differential class-based access to technology in the form of the digital divide. This digital divide has led to the second form of a knowledge gap, which is, as it sounds, an ongoing and increasing gap in information for those who have less access to technology. Simply put, students in well-funded schools receive more exposure to technology than students in poorly funded schools. Those students with more exposure gain more proficiency, which makes them far more marketable in an increasingly technology-based job market and leaves our society divided into those with technological knowledge and those without. Even as we improve access, we have failed to address an increasingly evident gap in e-readiness—the ability to sort through, interpret, and process knowledge (Sciadas 2003)[7]

With the cost of low-end computers dropping considerably in the 2000s, it led some to believe that the digital divide was naturally ending but this was very misleading. Most studies agree that there are minimal differences in internet use by adult men and adult women but this is largely because of the increase in the use of smartphones in recent years and research still indicates that technology use and internet access still vary by race, class and age in the United States.

Data from the Pew Research Center (2011) suggest the emergence of another divide. As technological devices get smaller and more mobile, larger percentages of minority groups (such as Latinos and African Americans) are using their phones to connect to the internet. In fact, about 50% of people in these minority groups connect to the web via such devices, whereas only one third of whites do. (Washington 2011). While it might seem that the internet is the internet, regardless of how you get there, there's a notable difference. Tasks like updating a resume or filling out a job application are much harder on a cell phone than on a wired computer in the home. As a result, the digital divide might mean no access to computers or the internet, but could mean access to the kind of online technology that allows for empowerment, not just entertainment (Washington 2011).[8]

THE DARK SIDE OF COMPUTER TECHNOLOGY
Surely We created man in the best of mold Then We reverted him to the lowest of the low. Except those who have faith and do righteous deeds [9]

Allah created Adam from earth and then breathed into Adam from His spirit (Ruh) which gave humans the ability to be spiritually higher than even the angels but it was conditional. Humans could only achieve that level of spirituality if they had faith and did righteous deeds. However, man was made from earth and there is a part of his or her nature (nafs) that clings to the earth and that is man's test. Remember, humans were created to worship their Creator, but those humans that worship money and power realized that they have to separate righteous people from divine guidance and they used a number of ways to do this. One way was to replace divine knowledge with human information. Another way was to corrupt man's nature. Part of humans worshiping their Creator was for them to be fruitful and multiply (have children). To insure that this happens, Allah has instilled in human beings physical desires and an attraction for members of the opposite sex. Human intimacy when done with the right intention, in the way that was prescribed by his Creator, is worship. But when done with the wrong intention, it can be turned into pornography. Pornographic movies probably came into existence shortly after the invention of moving pictures. But the technology of VCRs and DVDs were a major change and eventually the internet enabled people to have a limitless supply of pornographic videos without even leaving their homes.

"When you fight porn, you fight global capitalism,"...The venture capitalists, the banks, the credit card companies are all in this feeding chain. This is why you never see anti-porn stories. The media is implicated, it is financially in bed with these companies. Porn is part of this. Porn tells us we have nothing left as human beings – boundaries, integrity, desire, creativity, and authenticity. Women are reduced to three orifices and two hands. Porn is woven into the corporate destruction of intimacy and connectedness, and this includes the connectedness to the earth. If we were a society where we were whole, connected human beings in real communities, then we would not be able to look at porn. We would not be able to watch another human being tortured.[10]

It is estimated that the global income from pornography is $96 billion. It is also estimated that the United States' market accounts for $13 billion. There are "420 million internet porn pages, 4.2 million porn websites, and 68 million search engine requests for porn daily."..."The average kid gets his porn through the mobile phone."[11]

MAY ALLAH HELP US!

ENDNOTES

[1] Ali, Abdullah Yusuf, The Holy Quran, Page 431, Goodword Books, 2007

[2] Openstax, Introduction to Sociology 2E, Page 355, Rice University, 2016

[3] Rashid, Hakim, M. (Ideology and School Curriculum) Who Speaks For the Muslims In America, Pages 90 & 91, Sabur Abdul-Salaam, 2016

[4] Janssen, Sarah (Senior Editor), The World Almanac, Pages 376 & 377, Infobase, 2020

[5] Ibid. Page 379

[6] Openstax, Introduction to Sociology 2E, Page 158, Rice University, 2016

[7] Ibid. Page 158

[8] Ibid. Page 158

[9] Mawdudi, Sayyid Abul A'la, Towards Understanding the Quran, Page 1296, the Islamic Foundation, 2006

[10] Hedges, Chris, America: The Farewell Tour, Page 121, Simon and Schuster, 2018

[11] Ibid. Page 123

Chapter 5

THE ISLAMIC RENAISSANCE

When your Lord drew forth from the Children of Adam, From their loins, their descendants, and made them Testify concerning themselves, (saying): "Am I not your Lord (Who cherishes you and sustains you)?" They Said: "Yes! We do testify!"[1]

People have always known that Allah was their Creator and Sustainer but periodically they needed to be reminded, so Allah would send prophets and messengers to remind them that their main purpose was to worship the one and only God. Which means at some point in time, some of the Ancient Greeks believed in the existence and worshiped the One True God, the Creator of the heavens and the earth.

For We assuredly sent amongst every People a Messenger, (with the command), "Serve Allah, and eschew Evil": of the people were some whom Allah guided, and some on whom Error became inevitably (established).[2]

But it was after the Greeks had descended into paganism that they achieved outstanding accomplishments in the areas of literature and philosophy because those areas did not have to be based on divine revelations or scientific facts. Then when the Romans conquered the Greeks, they adopted the Greek's intellectual achievements. Initially they were both pagan civilizations so one could say that it was the blind leading the blind. However, in 305 C.E. (Christian Era), Constantine ascended to the throne and Christianity became the official religion of the Roman Empire. Since Christianity became the official religion of the state, many Romans outwardly converted while still being pagans at heart, which contributed to the paganization of Christianity, and Constantine became the one eyed man who was king in the land of the blind.[3]

The Prophet Muhammad (peace and blessings upon him) said, "Seeking knowledge is obligatory on every Muslim," and the early Muslims took this to heart and that is why they were able to achieve so much in the area of scientific knowledge because the Quran and the Prophet's traditions instructed them to study all of Allah's creation. And Abu Raihan Muhammad Al-Bayruni was one of the early Muslim scientists who best exemplified this. **Judge Al-Jisabouri reports, "I visited Abu Raihan when he was on his death-bed. He said to me, 'One day you told me about such and such a problem.' I said, 'you want me to explain it when you are in such a condition?' He said, 'Tell me. Is it not better that I leave this world with knowledge about this issue than dying while ignorant of it?'** Al-Bayruni died immediately after Al-Jisabouri left him.

> No wonder that our hero Al-Bayruni contributed so much to human knowledge. We are told that a simple listing of his written works covered more than sixty pages. A well known Orientalist (Max Meyerhaff, Legacy of Islam, 332) has this to say of our hero: "Abu Raihan Muhammad Al-Bayruni called 'The Master' (Al-Ustadh), a Persian physician, astronomer, mathematician, physicist, geographer and historian, is perhaps the most prominent figure in the phalanx of those universally learned Muslim scholars who characterize the Golden Age of Islamic Science..."[4]

Al-Bayruni holds a special place for students of Islam and Islamic history because he was a Muslim scientist who benefited both from Islamic guidance and scientific investigations, and together they strengthened his religious faith.

> He says..." My experience in the study of astronomy and geometry and experiments in physics revealed to me that there must be a Planning Mind of Unlimited Power. My discoveries in Astronomy showed that there are fantastic intricacies in the universe, which prove that there is a creative system and a meticulous control that cannot be explained through sheer physical and material causes."[5]

Abu Bakr Muhammad Ibn Zakariyya Ar-Razi was born in a town near Modern Tehran in 865 (C.E.). At a young age he became interested in alchemy and chemistry, philosophy, logic, mathematics and physics. However, he spent most of his life studying, practicing and writing about medicine. He became famous in the field of medicine and was appointed to the position of the head physician of the Rayy Hospital. Then during the reign of Adhud-Duddawlah, he was put in charge of the main hospital in Baghdad. A clear example of his intelligence, knowledge and willingness to think outside of the box was displayed when he was asked to build a new hospital. He had pieces of fresh meat placed in various locations of the city, and at a later period of time he checked the condition of the different pieces of meat and the piece that was least rotten was where he chose to build the hospital.

"His writings on small-pox and measles show originality and accuracy, and his essay on infectious diseases was the first scientific treatise on the subject." These are paraphrases of some comments made in the official bulletin of the World Health Organization about our hero, Abu Bakr Ar-Razi or Rhases, as he is better known in Western writings. (see Bulletin of WHO, May, 1970)[6]

✲ ✲ ✲ ✲ ✲ ✲ ✲ ✲ ✲ ✲

Abul-Waleed Muhammad Ibn Rushd (known as Averoes in the West) was born in 1126 (C.E.) in the City of Cordova. His father was a judge and his family was known for their appreciation of scholarship in general. Ibn Rushd studied religious law, medicine, mathematics and philosophy, which he is best known for in the West. At the age of 27 he helped to establish an Islamic educational institution in Marrakesh, Morocco. Ibn Tufail, another great Muslim philosopher, recommended that Ibn Rushd help with the translating, abridging and commenting on some works of Aristotle (in 1169 C.E.). After being appointed to the position of Judge (Qadi) in Seville, at the age of 44, that year he also translated and abridged Aristotle's book de Anima (Animal). Two years later he was transferred back to his birth place Cordova. During the next ten years he was both the Judge of that town and he wrote commentaries on the works of Aristotle including the Metaphysics. So Ibn Rushd was both a philosopher and religious scholar and he connected "true happiness" with mental and psychological health and religious faith. "True happiness for man can surely be achieved through mental and psychological health, and people can not enjoy psychological health unless they follow ways that lead to happiness in the Hereafter, and unless they believe in Allah and His Oneness."[7]

Ibn Al-Abbar said of our hero: "People went to him for consultation in medicine just as they did for consultation in legal matters and jurisprudence for our hero was another genius of encyclopedic scope. He spent a great part of his life as a judge and, partly, as a physician. Yet, he was known in the West for being the grand commentator on the philosophy of Aristotle whose influence penetrated the minds of even the most conservative of Christian ecclesiastes in the Middle Ages, including men like St. Thomas Aquinas.[8]

✴ ✴ ✴ ✴ ✴ ✴ ✴ ✴ ✴

<u>Ibn Khaldun</u> - The founding father of Sociology and the Science of History. Ibn Khaldun was born into a fairly wealthy family in Tunis, in the year 1332 (C.E.). However, his lineage goes back to Yemen but his family left Yemen traveling in the company of the army that conquered Spain.

Intellectually, our hero was well educated, having studied in Tunis first and Fez later the Qur'an, Prophet Muhammad's Ahadith and other branches of Islamic studies such as dialectical theology, Shari'ah (Islamic Law or Jurisprudence, according to the Maliki School of Thought). He also studied Arabic literature, philosophy, mathematics and astronomy. But we can safely say that our hero learnt very much from the school of life in which he actively participated, moving from place to place and from one royal court to another, sometimes at his own will, but often forced to do so by plotting rivals or despotic rulers.[9] It is obvious that both Ibn Khaldun's education and life experiences contributed to his views on history, culture and society which was beautifully expressed in his masterpiece "Al-Muqaddimah ('Prologue')." Ibn Khaldun's new and unique views had always attracted the attention of both Arab scholars and Western thinkers. Ibn Khaldun pioneered a new methodology in the study and writing of history. He subjected historical reports to reason and social and physical laws. He considered

the following four points worthy of consideration in studying and analyzing historical reports:
1. Relating events to each other through cause and effect.
2. Drawing analogy between the past and the present.
3. Taking into consideration the effect of the environment.
4. Taking into consideration the effect of inherited and economic conditions [10]

It is obvious from Ibn Khaldun's writing that Deen-al-Islam is a way of life and not just a religion. The role that Islam played in unifying the Arabs and the rapid development of the Muslim state clearly exemplifies this. He also points out the connection between religion and the state. When religion is replaced by injustice and despotism, they are clear signs that the state is in decline. And even though Ibn Khaldun studied philosophy, his preference for history may have been based on his opinion, "metaphysical philosophy has one advantage only, which is to sharpen one's wits."[11]

Ibn Khaldun pointed out that true progress and development comes through correct understanding of history, and the latter can only be achieved by observing the following:
1. **Absolute objectivity, which means that the historian should not be in any way prejudiced for or against anyone or any idea.**
2. **Confirmation and scrutiny of reported information. One should learn all one could about the historians whose reports one hears or reads. One should check their morals and trustworthiness before accepting their reports.**
3. **Not limiting history to the study of political and military news or to news about rulers and states. For History should include the study of all social, religious and economic conditions.**[12]

✼ ✼ ✼ ✼ ✼ ✼ ✼ ✼ ✼

It would be a very serious oversight if I did not include at least one of the outstanding female Muslim scholars who contributed to the Islamic scholarship during the Golden Age of Islam. **Karima bint Ahmad al Marwaziyya** (died 463 AH/1070 CE) was a scholar of Hadith and her specialty was the teaching of Sahih al Bukhari.

Born in the village of Kushmihan near Marw, Karima settled in

Mecca at an unknown juncture in her life. She never married and allegedly died at the age of one hundred lunar years (al-Dhabi, 1990-2000, vol. 31, pp. 180-181), Karima had superior knowledge of the lines of hadith transmission (isnad), for which she earned the honorific appellation "the musnida of the sacred precinct" (al-Dhahabi, 1990-2000, vol. 30, p. 274). She was known for her understanding (fahm) and knowledge (ilm), an indication that, she was a competent hadith evaluator.[13]

Karima's Scholarly Circle...Thirty-nine men and a single woman are documented to have transmitted on the authority of Karima...the Sahih (of al-Bukhari)...[14]

EUROPEAN ENLIGHTENMENT AND RELIGIOUS/CULTURAL ARROGANCE

The previously mentioned individuals were just some of the intellectual giants produced during the Islamic Renaissance. But you will not read about them in most Western history books. What some historians call the Middle-Ages, some scholars call the Golden Age of Islam. But what other historians call the Medieval Era was also known as Europes' Dark Ages. In the West the fall of the Roman empire marked the end of classical civilization and the beginning of the Medieval Era.[15]

In Western sources, European enlightenment was the result of religion being replaced by reason after the religious wars of the 17th Century.

During the Islamic Renaissance, the Quran and religion (Islam) was the primary motivation for intellectual pursuits, but in Europe, religion (Christianity) and the Bible were a hindrance to intellectual pursuits. The European masses could not read the Bible which was written in Latin at that time, and only the clergy and the European intellectuals were fluent in Latin, but even the European intellectuals were following religion blindly. The remarkable discoveries in science was also a contributing factor but most Western history books did not mention who the pioneers of those remarkable discoveries were.

> The religious wars of the 17th century, and the devastation they wrought, prompted many of Europe's intellectuals to begin questioning the notion that blind faith was the best route to wisdom and a contented life. Inspired by the remarkable

discoveries in science, or 'natural philosophy' as it was then known, educated people began to conclude that perhaps the scientific method, with its emphasis on the use of reason, could offer a surer path to knowledge, as well as to a more peaceful and harmonious existence. The idea that reason should be the principal guide in human affairs formed the basis of a movement known as the Enlightenment, which dominated European thought from the late 17th century until around 1800.[16]

He grants wisdom to whom He pleases; And he to whom wisdom is granted receives Indeed a benefit overflowing; but none will grasp the message except men of understanding. [17]

ENDNOTES

[1] Ali, Abdullah Yusuf, The Holy Quran, Page 112, Goodword Books, 2007
[2] Ibid. Page 181
[3] Nadwi, Sayyed Abul Hasan Ali, Islam and the World, Page 109, UK Islamic Academy, 2005
[4] Sieny, Mahmoud Esma'il, Heroes of Islam, Page 309, Darussalam Publishing House, 2000
[5] Ibid. Page 311
[6] Ibid. Page 312
[7] Ibid. Page 317
[8] Ibid. Page 315
[9] Ibid. Page 320
[10] Ibid. Page 321
[11] Ibid. Page 322
[12] Ibid. Pages 323 & 324
[13] Michalak-Pikulska, Barbara, Piela, Marek, Majtczak Tomasz, & Jagiellonian University Press, Oriental Languages and civilizations, Page 308, First Edition, KraKow. 2020
[14] Ibid. Page 309
[15] Woolf, Alex, A Short History of the World, Page 104, Metro Books, 2008
[16] Ibid. Page 170
[17] Ali, Abdullah Yusuf, The Holy Quran, Page 229, Goodword Books, 2007

Chapter 6

GREED AND CULTURAL/ RELIGIOUS ARROGANCE

Truly Man is, to his Lord, ungrateful and to that (fact) he bears witness (by his deeds) and violent is he in his love of wealth[1]

During the Golden Age of Islam, the Muslims were not only the most outstanding in the area of scientific knowledge, they were also the number one super power. It was the Quran that guided them in their scientific endeavors and the Quran and the Prophet's (pbuh) example that guided them in their submission to Allah which elevated them to their position of power. But as the saying goes "power can corrupt." When the love of Allah was replaced with the love of this life, the Muslims lost their position as a superpower. Europeans had no problem accepting and building on the scientific accomplishments of the Muslims, even though the Muslim's primary intellectual foundation stemmed from their religion. But most Europeans did not have the humility to study Islam even when science drove them away from Christianity. European's hatred of Muslims was so profound that it was given a name, "the Eastern Question."

> In fact the Eastern Question was nothing but an expression of hatred of the Christian powers of Europe against the Ottoman Empire. The Christian powers exploited every opportunity in their efforts to disintegrate the Ottoman Empire. Their efforts were on diplomatic, fiscal, religious, and cultural fronts. They took advantage wherever they found any weakness in the administration, intelligence system, military or naval power of the Ottomans.
>
> All the European powers were selfish, greedy and unscrupulous

but one aspect was common in all of them: prejudice and hatred of the Muslims.[2]

Empires do not rise and fall overnight, so let's look at some aspects of European history that contributed to the rise of the European powers. The 16th century was a transformational time in European and world history. Portugal, Spain, France, the Netherlands and England were the new world powers that would dominate this era by exploring far away parts of the world, opening new trade routes, and colonizing new lands. Important developments within Europe itself during this early modern period include the Reformation and religious conflicts, scientific discoveries and the growth of capitalism.[3]

The great era of European exploration that began in the 15th century arose primarily out of a desire to seek out new trade routes and partners. It was made possible by advances in cartography, navigation and shipbuilding. By the mid-1400s, much of the overland route between Europe and Asia was controlled by the Ottoman Turks. Muslims controlled the sea route between Asia and the Middle East, and Venice had a monopoly on the trade in eastern goods, including spices, between Middle Eastern ports and the rest of Europe. Other European powers were eager to break into this lucrative trade by finding a direct sea route to the Indies.[4]

Portugal's expedition to West Africa in 1415 led the way. Portuguese, by 1460, had established trade links with modern-day Sierra Leone, which provided the Portuguese with gold, spices and slaves. While the Portuguese were trying to find an Eastern sea route to the Indies, Christopher Columbus, a Genoese sailor, was convinced that there was a route going west across the Atlantic Ocean. Columbus was able to convince Queen Isabella of Spain and she sponsored his expedition in 1492. Columbus reached the land we now know as the Bahamas, but he thought he had reached India so he called the natives "Indians." The Spanish and Portuguese made guarding their colonies and sea routes in Central and South America a top priority, so the English and French focused on North America.[5]

Now let us discuss the Reformation. The Reformation was a powerful religious movement that split the church in Europe during the 16th century. It reduced the power of the Catholic church and caused a number of religious wars. It was a reaction to the perceived corruption and abuses of power during the late 15th and early 16th centuries. Martin Luther, a German monk, his "95 Theses" was a criticism of indulgences and grants sold by the Pope that would "supposedly" reduce the amount of time a person would have to spend in purgatory. By the end of 1519 about 250,000 copies of the "95 Theses" were in circulation. The laity were rebelling against papal authority because they wanted a greater role in the life of the church. A role they found in Protestantism.[6]

The racial prejudice of the Europeans prevented them from ever studying and considering the religion of Islam. But we the Muslims also have to take part of the blame for our neglecting to adequately convey the message of Islam to the Europeans. There are some Muslims who believe that we the Muslims living in the United States are doing the same thing today.

The racial prejudice of the Europeans also stood in the way. The barriers of hatred erected by the Crusades between the Christians and the Muslims, and the resulting ill-will of the Christian missionaries did a lot to entrench the antagonistic attitude of the West towards Islam. Part of the blame should, however, also be laid at the door of Muslim preachers, for they sadly neglected the opportunity of making such an important continent as Europe acquainted with the message of Islam, though all the resources of mighty Empires were at their disposal.[7]

THE GROWTH OF CAPITALISM IN EUROPE

Today capitalism is so pervasive in world economics, while at the same time has caused so much wealth inequality, people may wonder what preceded capitalism and why did people allow it to happen. This is a difficult question to answer, but in my opinion, the answer has to begin at the end of the 4th century when the Roman Empire permanently split into the Eastern and Western Roman Empires. Then less than one hundred years later, the Western Roman Empire came to an end.

By the 470s, the Western empire had shrunk to little more than Italy, and the emperors had become puppets of Germanic generals such as Ricimer, Orestes and Odoacer. The last emperor of the west was Romulus Augustulus. He was deposed in 476 by Odoacer, who proclaimed himself king of Italy.[8] Roman government, laws, commerce, culture and learning disappeared while trade and industry declined. Some historians consider the collapse of the Western Roman empire to be the end of the classical civilization and the start of the medieval era. Germanic tribes that settled in the former territories of the empire followed their traditional ways of life.[9]

Feudalism was the political and social system that grew out of the traditions of the Germanic tribes during Europe's early Middle Ages.

"The chieftain and the warriors of these tribes pledged loyalty to each other. The warriors fought for their chieftain and in return he rewarded them with estates and treasure...Under this system, land granted in the form of a fief remained the property of the lord: only the rights of the use were passed on. The fiefs comprised the land, the buildings on it; and the serfs who inhabited it; the vassal could receive what the land and peasants produced, including food and taxes."[10]

The eventual decline of the feudal system came as a result of the following three reasons.

1. "The fief, which had originally reverted to the lord on the death of a vassal, increasingly came to be seen as a hereditary entitlement, passed on from the vassal to his son. As such, the idea of a lord's ownership of the fief gradually fell away."
2. "At the same time, states grew more powerful and centralized. Monarchs could raise money to hire professional soldiers, and so were less dependent on their barons (warriors)."
3. "Kings demanded that allegiance be sworn to the state rather than to individual lords."

European urban life declined after the collapse of the Roman Empire and didn't begin to recover until the 10th century. During times of war, the local communities would seek protection within castle walls. As communities grew in size, urban centers developed around the castle and eventually became a town that was enclosed within a larger wall. Towns were the center of commercial activity. Once or twice a week there would be markets or fairs held in the town square. Farmers would sell their produce and craftspeople would sell their goods. The merchants and skilled workers formed trade associations called "guilds". These guilds were formed in order to protect their interests, lay down standards of quality, provide training and welfare benefits to their members. However, their primary purpose was to protect their members from external competition.[11]

Banks and credit became a necessity as towns and cities became more prosperous. Buyers and sellers were having to handle larger sums of money which was both inconvenient and dangerous. Necessity being the mother of inventions, the first European system of credit was established. A system of credit necessitated good record keeping, and the Italian mathematician, Luca Pacioli is credited with developing the first system of bookkeeping which gave way to the accountancy profession. Banks began to appear in Northern Italian communities by the end of the 12th century. These banks greatly facilitated commerce and trade because they could store money safely, arrange loans and transfers of funds between accounts over long distances. The Medieval era's leading bank belonged to the Medici in Florence (1391-1494). In addition to handling the finances of the papacy and several of Europe's royal families, it also helped to fund military campaigns and collect taxes for its royal customers.[12]

MERCHANT CAPITALISM PRECEDED MODERN INDUSTRIAL CAPITALISM

…The growth of merchant capitalism. This early, pre-industrial form of Capitalism developed in European cities such as Venice, Antwerp, Genoa, Amsterdam and London, where sophisticated banking and credit systems were established, providing finance for long-distance trade, as well as for kings and governments. By the late 18th century, with the development of industrial methods of production and the arrivals of factories, merchant capitalism gave way to modern, industrial capitalism.[13]

Contrary to Ronald Reagan's "trickle down economics" claim, Thomas Piketty in his book 'Capital in the Twenty-First

Century,' makes the very insightful claim that capital, by its very nature, its rate of return is greater than the overall rate of economic growth. Modern history shows that wealth grows faster than the rest of the economy which is a major contributing factor to wealth inequality. "The imbalance isn't a glitch in the system but rather the natural product of the global economy left to its own devices."[14]

Europeans and Americans have spent five centuries conquering, plundering, exploiting, and polluting the earth in the name of human progress. They used their technological superiority to create the most efficient killing machines on the planet, directed against anyone and anything, especially indigenous cultures, which stood in their way. They stole and hoarded the planet's wealth and resources. They believed that this orgy of blood and gold would never end, and they still believe it. They do not understand that the dark ethic of ceaseless capitalist and imperialist expansion is dooming the exploiters as well as the exploited.[15]

Capitalism contributed to making the United States the richest country in the world with the highest number of billionaires and the highest number of imprisoned people. Islam has a superior economic system but because the Islamic economic system is not being used by any Muslim country, there is no example of the Islamic economic system for the non-Muslim world to see.

MAY ALLAH FORGIVE US.

ENDNOTES

[1] Ali, Abdullah Yusuf, The Holy Quran, Page 436, Goodword Books, 2007

[2] Ahmed, Hasanuddin, A Brief History of Islam, Page 415, Goodword Books, 2010

[3] Woolf, Alex, A Short History of the World, Page 152, Metro Books, 2008

[4] Ibid. Page 154

[5] Ibid. Page 154

[6] Ibid. Page 156

[7] Nadwi, Sayyed Abul Hasan Ali, Islam and the World, Page 119, UK Islamic Academy, 20005

[8] Woolf, Alex, A Short History of the World, Page 75, Metro Books, 2008

[9] Ibid. Page 104

[10] Ibid. Page 112

[11] Ibid. Page 116

[12] Ibid. Page 117

[13] Ibid. Page 168

[14] Stangler, Cole, Tipping Point, Page 28, The Nation Magazine, June 1/8, 2020

[15] Hedges, Chris, America: The Farewell Tour, Page 43, Simon & Schuster, 2018

Chapter 7

CAUSE AND EFFECT

On no soul does Allah place a burden greater than it can bear. It gets every Good that it earns, and it suffers every Ill that it earns. [1]

One of the reasons empires rise and fall is because oppression tends to humble people, so some of the oppressed will pray and ask God to free them from the oppression of their tyrannical rulers and their prayers may be granted allowing them to overthrow their tyrannical rulers, enabling them to rise to power and become the replacement of their oppressive rulers, until they or their descendants become oppressive rulers. Some of America's founding fathers were excellent con men. They ensured that Americans would have freedom of speech and eventually produced public schools that turned out individuals who were only functionally literate. Most could read newspapers and fill out job applications but would not read books. The television and movies would eventually become the creator of their reality. Even among the literate in the schools of higher education, it was the grants and endowments of the rich and large corporations that guided the pen of the college professors. Becoming millionaires by exploiting the American masses was not enough, why be satisfied exploiting the American masses when globalization will enable the millionaires to exploit the world's masses and become billionaires. Then books like The World Is Flat, convinced those working people that read books that globalization was a good thing, at least for a while.

GLOBALIZATION

Globalization refers to the process of integrating governments, cultures, and financial markets through international trade into a single world market. Often, the process begins with a single motive, such as market expansion (on the part of a corporation) or increased access to health care (on the part of a non-profit organization). But usually there is a snowball effect, and globalization becomes a mixed bag of economic, philanthropic, entrepreneurial, and cultural efforts.

> Some globalization efforts can be extremely complex. Take for example the North American Free Trade Agreement (NAFTA). Canada, the United States and Mexico agreed to much freer trade opportunities that excluded normal tariffs and import laws, making it easier to conduct international trade. Politicians and economists presented all the potential trade opportunities but neglected to mention the possible problems like decreases in job opportunities. Once jobs could be outsourced to workers in Mexico who were eager to do the work for much less money, American workers became less competitive. Most Americans had to settle for lower paying jobs with less job security.[2]

> History and politics point out that expanded trade gives the consumer cheaper goods and services, but the ones who benefit the most are the investors and the executives. You might say that the American consumer came to the realization that I do not need a television in every room. By 2014 most Americans no longer supported trade-opening agreements and, according to polls, in 2015 most Americans were opposed to the Trans-Pacific Partnership (TPP).[3]

When Bernie Sanders and Donald Trump began pointing out some of the negative aspects of globalization, then books had to be published convincing those Americans that read books (the intellectuals), that globalization is not new and that the pros outweigh the cons, and it does for the top one percent. I think Jeffrey Sachs (The Ages of Globalization) is an extremely intelligent economist who has devoted his life to trying to make the lives of people better, but sometimes scholars who see the glass half-full are used to paint a picture of reality that people will see-through rose-tinted lenses.

> Jeffery Sachs stresses the importance of studying history to understand the globalization changes (which sometimes came quickly and violently) over the past 70,000 years. Assuming that through studying history, it should help us understand and manage globalization in the twenty-first century.[4]

> Let us keep our eye on five big questions. First, what have been the main drivers of global-scale change? Second, how do geography, technology, and institutions interact?

How do changes in one region diffuse to others? Fourth, how have these changes affected global interdependence? Fifth, what lessons have we glean from each age to help us meet our challenges today?[5]

I was very surprised that none of the key questions mentioned the relationship between human greed, poverty and hunger. However, he does mention the human misery caused by Britain's colonialism and America's slavery and it would be difficult to say which of the two was the worst.

THE PAINFUL REALITY OF COLONIZATION

Recent years have seen a resurgence in nostalgia for the British empire. High profile books such as Niall Fuguson's Empire: How Britain Made the Modern World, and Bruce Gilley's The Last Imperialist, have claimed that British colonialism brought prosperity and development to India and other colonies. Two years ago, a YouGov poll found that 32 percent of people in Britain are actively proud of the nation's colonial history.

This rosy picture of Colonialism conflicts dramatically with the historical record. According to research by the economic historian Robert C. Allen, extreme poverty in India increased under British rule, from 23 percent in 1810 to more than 50 percent in the mid-20th century. Real wages declined during the British colonial period, reaching a nadir in the 19th century, while famines became more frequent and more deadly. Far from benefitting the Indian people, colonialism was a human tragedy with few parallels in recorded history.

While the precise number of deaths is sensitive to the assumptions we make about baseline mortality, it is clear that somewhere in the vicinity of 100 million people died prematurely at the height of British colonialism. This is among the largest policy-induced mortality crises in human history. It is larger than the combined number of deaths that occurred during all famines in the Soviet Union, Maoist China, North Korea, Pol Pot's Cambodia, and Mengistu's Ethiopia.[6]

Sachs also mentioned that it took humanity a long time to break free of poverty and hunger.[7]

But the reality is that poverty and hunger still exist. In the United States the richest country in the world, 38.1 million people (11.8 percent of the population) were still living below the poverty line in the year 2018.[8]

Sachs also points out how the spread of industrialization contributed to the rise of urbanization and living standards, but it was a slow process even in the developed nations, and in many cases, the boost to the middle-class was only temporary.

PROBLEMS OF URBANIZATION

In general "urbanization" is the study of the social, political and economic relationships in cities. But to understand the problems of urbanization in 19th century America, you have to look at the living conditions of the people. One could begin with the absence of adequate housing. The newcomers were not able to afford individual houses or good apartments, instead they were forced to live in the cramped and filthy tenements, which were built in large numbers after the 1880's. Tenements were usually four to six stories high with each floor having several poorly ventilated and dimly lit family units consisting of two to four rooms. Many tenement rooms had no outside exposure at all. One observer describing the Italian section of New York said the following, "Here the mud, dirt and filth, the stinking humidity, the incumbrances, the disorder of the streets are beyond description."

Millions of new urban dwellers suffered from the inadequate public services of running water, garbage disposal and general sanitation. Hogs ran lose eating the refuse in the city streets, as late as the 1870's. The garbage was often dumped in the nearest river or lake with no regards or precautions for general health. Inadequate water was often the norm and the danger of fire was always present.[9]

Land, slavery and capitalism enabled America to become the richest country in the world but globalization took most of the wealth from the middle-class and put it into the hands of the top one percent. Anderson, Indiana was once a prosperous city, it had a General Motors plant that employed 25,000 workers. One in every three people worked for General Motors. But once the North American Free Trade Agreement (NAFTA) was implemented, the GM plant relocated to Mexico in 2006. Parts of Anderson became a ghost town. The population fell from 70,800 to 55,000. "Schools, churches, supermarkets, restaurants, dry cleaners, and furniture stores were closed and boarded up.[10]

People who do not believe in a Supreme Being who has a master plan often think that life is arbitrarily filled with ups and downs, partly because they sometimes see evil people who have received all the worldly benefits, while many good decent people who are living lives of pain and misery. What they fail to understand is that the perfect results of cause and effects will ultimately come in the Hereafter but obviously that requires a person having religious faith. However, sometimes signs are given that serve as a protection for those who are innocent and a punishment for the evil doers, so perhaps they may mend their ways. During the time of the African slave trade, because of the disease of malaria, West Africa was known as the "white man's grave."[11]

Corruption has spread on land and sea as a result of what people's hands have done, So that God may cause them to taste the consequences of some of their deeds and perhaps they might return to the Right Path.[12]

ENDNOTES

[1] Ali, Abdullah Yusuf, The Holy Quran, Page 31, Goodword Books, 2007

[2] Abdul-Salaam, Sabur, Rise and Fall of Great Empires – Black Lives Matter, Page 99, Sabur Abdul-Salaam, 2021

[3] Ibid. Page 100

[4] Sachs, Jeffery D., The Ages of Globalization, Page 1, Columbia University Press, 2020

[5] Ibid. Page 2

[6] Sullivan, Dylan, and Hickel, Jason, How British Colonialism killed 100 Million Indians In 40 Years, ALJAZEERA, 2 December 2022

[7] Sachs, Jeffery D., The Ages of Globalization, Page 7, Columbia University Press, 2022

[8] Janssen, Sarah (Senior Editor), The World Almanac, Page 50, Infobase, 2020

[9] Abdul-Salaam, Sabur, Rise and Fall of Great Empires – Black Lives Matter, Pages 60 & 61, Sabur Abdul-Salaam, 2021

[10] Hedges, Chris, America: The Farewell Tour, Page 90, Simon & Schuster, 2018

[11] Sachs, Jeffery D., The Ages of Globalization, Page X, Columbia University Press, 2020

[12] Khattab, Mustafa, The Clear Quran, Page 228, Book of Signs Foundation, 2016

Chapter 8

CULTURE/SOCIAL NORMS

O' Prophet! We have sent you As a witness, and a deliverer of good news, and a warner, and a caller to the way of God. [1]

The word "culture" is another word that is used to describe a peoples' way of life. "The word 'culture' comes from the Latin 'cultura' which is a derivative of the verb 'colere' meaning 'tending' or 'cultivation'…However, culture in anthropological usage, may be defined as 'the way of life of a specific group."[2] The culture of most of the world today is that of Western Europe and America. It was exported to the remainder of the world during the period of European colonization and continued during the neo-colonial era by way of indirect rule. In the twentieth century, Western culture has been promoted on a massive scale through the far reaching effects of the media. Today, it is not surprising to find in the pages of National Geographic pictures of South American Indian youths in loin cloth in the middle of the Amazon wearing baseball caps with a Nike logo or Mongolian horsemen in the middle of the Gobi desert wearing striped Adidas sweat pants and Reebok trainers.[3]

Most of the nations in the West have democratic political systems, but it also impacts all social norms. "Western democracy reaches beyond the confines of government and affects all phases of human relations."[4]

So in the twentieth century the United States decided that its' mission 'supposedly" was to go around the world spreading democracy (American culture). America's justification for doing this was that it considered western culture superior to all other cultures.

This assumption is based on Darwin's Theory of Evolution. The evolutionary process "refines and improves" human beings and their societies. From the savage ape-like origins, to the civilized twentieth century human being. Using "survival of the fittest" as a yardstick, after World War II, America and other western nations were at the top of the human pecking order.

However, America did not want to just spread democracy (government of the people, by the people and for the people), they really wanted to spread "secular democracy." In a secular democracy, religion should have no say in public education and all other matters of civil policies. This was a radical change because most of the world had some type of religious belief and you could see the influence of their religious beliefs in some of their governing laws, and it wasn't until the Renaissance when the philosophy of "Humanism" developed and the Western world began to become more secularized and it has become a permanent part of modern history. [5]

The bottom line is that human beings can either worship their Creator or worship something else. True religion teaches that man's primary purpose is to worship their Creator, which enables them to live righteous lives on earth and a life of eternal bliss in the Hereafter. However, in secular democracies (or in other words "liberal democracies), humans are considered a product of the evolutionary process, which makes them not much different from other animals whose primary purpose is the acquisition of the necessities of life. So one could say that modern man's purpose is to "eat, drink and be merry for tomorrow you may die." [6]

Theoretically, democracy as a way of life is based on three principles: The first principle is "equality". The rationalist humanist perspective acknowledges human differences such as class, race, sex, nationality and religion, but considers all humans equal because they share the common trait of the ability to reason. The second principle is "rational empiricism". Rational empiricism implies full confidence in human reason and experience. This means that humans using their ability to reason and their life experience, they could deduce what is best for human society. But the fact that the American Constitution, article 1, section 2 stated that black men (who were slaves at the time), for political and economic reasons, were considered 3/5s of a white man, this is a clear indication that human reason and experience failed to convince America's founding fathers to treat black men in a fair and just manner, but instead made laws according to their own sectarian or class interests. The third principle is referred to as "discussion and consent", and this principle clearly shows the inconsistency in democratic rule. This principle shows that some laws are based on "social norms", the norms of society at any given time. So, "what is good today can become evil tomorrow and vice versa." There are numerous examples of this in American history, the following is just one.

> Another classic case in point, is that of the homosexual onslaught in the latter part of the 20th century. If the average Westerner were asked about his or her view of homosexuality in the 50's and 60's, they would immediately respond that it was sick, degenerate, perverse, etc.. If they were religious they might even quote the Bible in which it is referred to as "an abomination unto the Lord." Psychiatrists of that period included it in their main reference works as a mental illness with suggested treatments ranging from shock therapy to drug therapy. However, if the same question was asked in the 70's and early 80's, the response would have been that homosexuality is a personal choice, an alternative lifestyle, "different strokes for different folks", etc.. Consequently, homosexuality has been stricken from the Psychiatrist's Bible, only to be replaced by another illness called "homophobia".[7]

When a society becomes a secular democracy, it becomes necessary to change those laws that were based on religious values. The sexual revolution of the fifties and sixties made it necessary to change some American laws. Adultery had been a punishable crime but when American lawmakers analyzed fornication and marriage, they concluded that the marriage certificate (a piece of paper) was the only difference between the two. In a secular democracy (aka liberal democracy) an activity should not be made unlawful based on the Ten Commandments.

> <u>Morality</u> - Moral is that which is connected with the principles of right and wrong conduct and morality is the quality of conforming to the principles of good conduct. The question which remains is: "How do we define right or wrong or good

conduct?" Right and wrong may vary according to the perspective from which one views an action.

Democratic Morality - In the democratic system, moral values are set according to the preference of the majority. Consequently, it is inherently unstable and incomplete.

Islamic Morality - The Islamic system of morality is a complete system that governs human relations with God, with other humans and with the environment. It is morally good to worship God and morally evil to worship His creation. Preservation of one's life is morally good, while suicide is morally evil. Taking an animal's life for food or for clothing is morally good while killing an animal for sport is considered morally evil.[8]

ENDNOTES

[1] Khattab, Mustafa, The Clear Quran, Page 238, Book of Signs Foundation, 2016
[2] Philips, Abu Ameenah Bilal, The Clash of Civilizations (An Islamic View), Page 9, Al-Hidaayah Publishing and Distribution LTD, 2007
[3] Ibid. Page 10
[4] Ibid. Page 25
[5] Ibid. Page 22
[6] Ibid. Page 24
[7] Ibid. Pages 27-28
[8] Ibid. Pages 65-67

Chapter 9

A FIFTY-YEAR JOURNEY TO FIND OUT WHY?

He it is Who Created you from dust, then from a sperm drop, then from a clot; then he brings you out as an infant, then causes you to grow into full maturity, and then causes you to grow further so that you may reach old age, while some of you He recalls earlier. All this is in order that you may reach an appointed term and that you may understand (the truth).[1]

As a child while attending public school in the Bronx section of New York City, every year during Negro History Week (it was eventually changed to Black History Month), they would show the movie, The Jackie Robinson Story. When Branch Rickey, the general manager of the Brooklyn Dodgers, approached Jackie Robinson to consider being the first black player in major league baseball, even though some white spectators would curse at him, spit at him and even make violent threats.

> In a famous three-hour exchange on August 28, 1945, Rickey asked Robinson if he could face the racial animus without taking the bait and reacting angrily…Robinson was aghast: 'are you looking for a Negro who is afraid to fight back?' Rickey replied that he needed a Negro player 'with guts enough not to fight back.'[2]

I guess the objective was to make black children proud to be black but what it did for me was to start me on my journey of becoming a social scientist because I wanted to know what Jackie Robinson or black people in general had done to make white people hate us so much.

Even though my journey that led to my becoming a social scientist began when I was in elementary school, I was not a good student, nor did I like school. However, since it was a journey that my Creator had decreed for me, He provided me with the necessary milestones I needed to get from one place to the next. My first important milestone was my home in the Bronx where I spent the first twelve years of my life. Residing in the home was my mother's Aunt Edith, her husband Uncle Joe, my cousin Edie who was six years older than me and my brother Sonny who was four years older than me. We had the basement apartment of an all white apartment building but we were allowed to live there because Uncle Joe was the superintendent of the building. My second milestone was when I was four years old and a Jewish family moved into a first floor apartment and they had a son who was a year younger than me.

> **I began spending more time in their apartment than I did in mine. As far as the mother was concerned, I could not wear out my welcome. The boy (we can call him David) was a spoiled brat, so having a playmate helped his mother maintain her sanity…I also would eat there regularly, which I thoroughly enjoyed because his mother was an excellent cook. I remember when the movie The Ten Commandments was released, David's mother took us to see it. Because the movie was very long they showed half and then had an intermission…However, it was during the intermission that I noticed that all the other children in the movie theater were white (and probably the majority was Jewish) but David's family always treated me like I was one of the family so I didn't feel uncomfortable at all.[3]**

I remember when the movie The Ten Commandments was released, David's mother took us to see it. I didn't realize it at the time but that movie planted the seeds of One God and prophet-hood in my heart. As a young child I went to Sunday school and was taught about Jesus and the concept of the Trinity but it never made sense to me. Why did God have to have His son crucified in order for God to forgive humans of their sins? It seemed like God had someone over Him who told Him, the only way I will let you forgive the Humans is if you crucify your son. But in the movie The Ten Commandments, it was made clear that there is an All Powerful God and the Prophet Moses was [one of] his human representatives.

My next milestone was my move to Philadelphia to live with my mother, stepfather and siblings when I was twelve years old. My early life included some contrasting experiences, the following are two of them.

Contrast number five, in New York I had always been the youngest child in the house, the baby, but in Philadelphia I already had my younger brother Wakil, and three younger sisters, Ella, Francine and Lorraine, and my sister Gail was born a month after I moved there.

Contrast number six, moving from a white neighborhood in the Bronx to South Philadelphia or the Hood. Some of my classmates in the Bronx thought I was tough, but in South Philly you had some "real" tough guys. I moved to Philly in June of 1959 at the beginning of the summer vacation. My mother and stepfather had just bought a five bedroom house on 15th Street, right off of Ellsworth Street, 1122 South 15th Street to be exact. My family would live in that house for the next fifty years. However, for the next two months my world consisted of four blocks: the block that I lived on and the three intersecting blocks. This is noteworthy because in New York my Friends and I would go to the shows at the world famous Apollo Theater or take a one and a half hour subway ride to Coney Island on any given summer day, but at 12 years old in Philadelphia, it was as if I was going through my second childhood.

Another important point that needs to be made is that my new four block world was a black working/middle class neighborhood, but three blocks away on 16th and Federal Street, you were in the heart of the hood. [4]

Initially I went to Barrett Junior High School and then in 1965 I graduated from South Philadelphia High School. In the 1960s, if you did not have a college deferment, a young black man was almost guaranteed to be drafted into the army. So after graduation in 1965, I enlisted into the army and was honorably discharged with the rank of Specialist Fourth Class in 1968. As a young child I had occasionally seen Uncle Joe get on his knees and say his prayers before going to bed. So I too began saying my prayers before going to bed and I did this up until the age of 19. During the black consciousness era of the second half of the 1960s, while I was in the Army, I learned that African slaves were not permitted to practice their religion and were only allowed to practice the religion of the slave masters. So at the age of 19 I stopped praying.

My next milestone came upon my return to Philadelphia after leaving the military. A good friend of mine gave me a copy of The Autobiography of Malcolm X. Malcolm's autobiography had a strong impact on me in two ways: first it provided me with a powerful, streetwise male role model. Secondly, it was my first introduction to black consciousness and some aspects of Sunni Islam. I then began reading a lot and not long afterwards I moved back to New York.

MY SEARCH FOR SPIRITUAL GUIDANCE

Reading Malcolm's autobiography increased my social, political and spiritual consciousness.

Malcolm's biography did not describe the true religion of Islam in any detail, but it did give a very powerful description of the brotherhood that he had experienced during his pilgrimage to Makkah in 1964. Obviously, for young African-American men who grew-up in the US during the 1950s and the 1960s, it would have a profound impact on our hearts and minds. However, I was not religious at all at the time, nor was I looking for religion. Then I experienced a very defining moment in my life: I became sick and began throwing up all the food that I ate. After doing this for two or three days, I went to the hospital. The doctors gave me a very thorough examination, and I was given an appointment to come back and find out the results. While at home, I was experiencing serious stomach pains. At one point, it almost seemed unbearable. When I was a child, I used to say my prayers every night before going to bed. However, I stopped praying at the age of 19.

So there I was at the age of 25, not having said a prayer in six years, falling to my knees and beginning to pray. I asked my Creator to forgive me and please help me in my time of need. The pain immediately became bearable...At that point, I knew I needed to add a spiritual element to my life. But what? I had grown up as a Christian, and yet had no desire to return to the church. I had a certain attraction to Islam, but was not ready to make the commitment that it would require.

In my heart, I knew that this certainty (the certainty that I needed) could come only from the Quran. And so I bought a Quran. When I say I bought a Quran, I mean that I bought a Quran that included the English translation, because the Quran was revealed in Arabic and consists of the exact words of Allah conveyed to the Prophet Muhammad by the Angel Jibreel (Gabriel). Since I did not know Arabic, I needed an English translation…I became totally convinced that my Creator was the author of the Quran, because it told me things about myself that only my Creator could know. Paradise and the Hellfire became realities for me, so I could no longer sit on the fence. I had to make a choice. So my choice was to go to the mosque and say the testimony of faith (shahadah): 'I bear witness that there is nothing (and no one) worthy of worship except Allah, and I bear witness that Muhammad is the Messenger of Allah.'[5]

ISLAM AND UNIVERSAL PEACE

Islam is not a religion, it is a total way of life. So in addition to praying five times a day, fasting the month of Ramadan, giving the annual charity and making the pilgrimage to Mecca at least once, a Muslim is also expected to marry and have children, insha Allah, and to live a life that is pleasing to Allah with the hope of spending eternity in Paradise. So this was my intention (nothing special) until I read the book Islam and Universal Peace, written by Sayyid Qutb, and this was my next milestone.

Sayyid Qutb was an intelligent but average Egyptian educator and writer until he spent some time in the United States. By Islamic standards, the United States was a very immoral country and unless a strong effort was made to bring the Muslims back to the Islamic way of life based on the Quran and the Prophet Muhammad's example, Egyptian life would continue on the path of imitating life in the West. So he spent the remainder of his life trying to reverse that trend.

Michael Hart points out in his book The 100, that the Prophet Muhammad was the most influential person in Human history. But the Prophet Muhammad was Allah's final Prophet and he received divine revelations from Allah so of course it was expected that he would have been able to do miraculous things. However, Sayyid Qutb in his book Islam And Universal Peace, points out that in spite of the fact that humans are a mere speck in the universe, a believer has the ability to connect himself to the All Powerful Creator, and through the believer's submission, he too may be given the ability to do miraculous things. At that point I had no idea what Allah had decreed for me, but I no longer limited my life's aspirations because I knew that Allah is able to do all things.

MILESTONES

Sayyid Qutb's book Islam And Universal Peace changed my life but his book MILESTONES taught me an even more life changing lesson. All Muslims believe Laa elaha il-lal-lah (there is nothing worthy of worship except Allah), however, only a small percentage of the Muslims have a deep understanding of its meaning. It wasn't until I read Milestones that I began to have an understanding of how profound that statement really is.

All Muslims realize that there is only One God, but very few of us realize the weight of the responsibility that we have inherited from the Prophet Muhammad to convey that message to others and why it is so important. Allah used an incident in the life of the Prophet and the blind man Ibn Umm Maktoom to show that a persons' relationship with Allah should be the yardstick used when evaluating someone because humans were created to worship Allah, so it is only through our submission/worship and repentance, that we can live a life that is pleasing to Allah. A person's family, position or wealth are meaningless to Allah unless they enable him or her to be a better Muslim.

Sayyid Qutb says the following concerning Surah Abasa in his commentary, In The Shade Of The Quran:

"Its first part treats a certain incident which took place in the early days of Islam. The Prophet (PBUH) was busy with a few dignitaries of the tribe of Quraish, explaining to them the message of Islam, when Ibn Umm Maktoom, a poor blind man, interrupted him. Unaware that the Prophet was busy with those people, the blind man asked him repeatedly to teach him some verses of the Quran. The Prophet (peace be upon him) was not very pleased at this interruption. He frowned and turned away from Ibn Umm Maktoom. This Surah opens by criticizing the Prophet's behavior in this incident. It lays down clearly the values and principles upon which Islamic society is founded and states the true nature of the message of Islam. 'He frowned and turned his back when the blind man came to him. How could you tell? He might have sought to purify himself.

He might have been forewarned, and the reminder might have profited him. But to the one who considered himself self-sufficient you were all attention. Yet the fault would not be yours if he remained uncleansed. As to him who comes to you with zeal and with a feeling of fear in his heart—him you ignore and busy yourself with trifles. No indeed! This is an admonition; let him who will bear it in mind. It is written on honored pages, exalted, purified by the hands of noble and devout scribes." - Surah 80:1-15

The Divine instructions that followed this incident are much more far reaching than appears at first sight. They are indeed a miracle. These instructions, the principles they seek to establish and the change they aim to accomplish in human society are, perhaps the first and greatest miracle of Islam. But the instructions are made here as a direct comment on a single incident. It is a part of the Quranic method to make of isolated incidents in order to lay down fundamental and permanent principles... They constitute the truth which Islam and the earlier Divine religions seek to plant in human life.

The point at issue here is not merely how an individual or a class of people should be treated. This is indeed the significance of the Quranic comment on the incident itself, taken in isolation. The heart of the matter is, however, something far more important. It is: how should people evaluate everything in their lives? From where they derive their values and their standards for such an evaluation.

What the Divine instructions contained in the opening part of the surah seek to establish is that men must base their values and standards on Divine considerations, laid down by Allah.[6]

A Muslim is a student from the cradle to the grave, so after many years of studying, my book Rise and Fall of Great Empires – Black Lives Matter describes what black people did to make some white people hate us so much. Our crime was the color of our skin, but the majority of white people in the 99% were being manipulated by the 1%. My teacher Muhammad Qutb, the brother of Sayyid Qutb, told us in class one day that there are two categories of unbelievers, those that set themselves up as gods (the 1%) and those that accept them as gods.

ENDNOTES

[1] Mawdudi, Sayyid Abul A'la, Toward Understanding The Quran, Pages 970-971, The Islamic Foundation, 2006
[2] Robinson, Jackie, Negro Leagues and Major Leagues Prospects, Page 33, Wikipedia, 1995
[3] Abdul-Salaam, Sabur, Spiritual Journey of An American Muslim, Page 5, Sabur Abdul-Salaam, 2013
[4] Ibid. Pages 15-16
[5] Ibid. Pages 61-63
[6] Abdul-Salaam, Sabur, Who Speaks For the Muslims in America, Pages 59-60, Sabur Abdul-Salaam, 2016

Chapter 10

DIGNITY OF WORK

Among His signs is this, that He sends The Winds, as heralds of Glad Tidings, giving you a taste of His (Grace and) Mercy–that the ships may sail (majestically) by His Command and that you may seek of His Bounty: in order that you may be grateful. [1]

Some people regard certain kinds of work or professions contemptible, but a Muslim can earn his livelihood through agriculture, trade, industry or any other profession or employment as long as it does not involve doing, supporting, or propagating anything unlawful. [2] In other words, a Muslim is not permitted to earn money in any way that he may want to, but instead he is restricted to using lawful methods based on the criterion of the overall well-being of the society. [3]

Earning through Agriculture - Many places in the Quran it points out that the earth is spacious and fertile, suitable for cultivation and production, and these are just a few of the blessings that Allah has bestowed on His creation.

Then let man look at his food, how We pour forth water in abundance, then We split the earth into fragments and produce therein corn and grapes and nutritious plants. (80:24-28)

And He has spread out the earth for (His) creatures. In it is fruit, and date palms with spathes, and husked corn, and scented herbs. Then which of the favors of your Lord will you deny? (55:10-13)

And the Prophet Muhammad (pbuh) said:

When a Muslim plants a plant, anything eaten of it or stolen from it, until the Day of Resurrection is accounted as a charity for him. (Sahih Muslim)[4]

Industries and Professions - Food is a necessity of life so obviously agriculture is an essential pursuit for every society. So Islam encourages it by pointing out its benefits both in this life and the Hereafter. However, Islam also points out that not everyone should restrict their livelihood to agriculture because that would expose the Muslims to the dangers of defeat and humiliation at the hands of the more materialistic and aggressive nations.

Thus, in addition to agriculture, the Muslim must develop such industries, crafts and professions as are essential for the life of a community, for the strength of a free and powerful nation, and for the posterity and wealth of a country. As the great scholars and jurists have explained, the essential industries and professions are not merely permitted by the Islamic Shari'ah, they are in fact an obligation of the Muslim community as a whole. Such obligations are termed "the obligations of sufficiency" (fard kifiyah); that is to say, the Muslim community must include among its members people engaged in every essential science, industry and profession in numbers sufficient to meet its needs.[5]

The Quran says:

> **And We send down iron, in which there is great strength and benefits for mankind...**(57:25)

The Quran says concerning the Prophet Daoud (David in the Bible):

> **And We made iron soft for him (commanding): make thou coats of mail and balance the links...** (34:10-11)

> **And We taught him the art of making garments (of mail) to protect you from your violence. Will you then be thankful?**[6]

Trade - Both the Quran and the traditions of the Prophet Muhammad encourages the Muslims to engage in trade and commerce, and to travel seeking the bounties of Allah. The use of merchant ships for transporting import/export goods throughout the world is another blessing from Allah. The Quran says:

And among His signs is that He sends the winds as heralds of good tidings and in order that you may taste His mercy, and that the ships may sail by His command and that you may seek of His bounty, and in order that you may be thankful. [7]

Salaried Employment - The Muslim is free to seek employment in the service of the government, an organization, or an individual as long as he is able to do his work satisfactorily and carry out his duties. However, he is not permitted to seek a job for which he is unfit, especially if the job carries judicial or executive authority.

Abu Hurairah reported (in an authentic tradition) the Prophet (pbuh) as saying,

Woe to the rulers, the leaders and the trustees! On the Day of resurrection some people will wish that they could be suspended between heaven and earth rather than having had the burden of their responsibilities. [8]

Prohibited Forms of Work - Before concluding this chapter I felt it necessary to briefly mention some of the forbidden forms of work or sources of income.

Industries and Professions Condemned by Islam - Islam has prohibited certain professions and industries to its followers because they are harmful to the beliefs, morals, honor, or good manners of the society. [9]

Prohibited crops: The growing of hashish because it is an intoxicant and the growing of tobacco because it can cause cancer. And it is not a valid excuse for a muslim merchant, because he intends to sell it only to non-Muslims. It is also not permitted for Muslims to raise pigs to cell to Christians or to grow grapes to be used in the making of wine or other fruits to make any type of intoxicant. [10]

Prostitution: (the Quran says)

...And do not force your slave-girls to prostitution if they desire chastity, in order that you may seek the pleasures of this world's life... (24:33)

Dancing and Other Erotic Arts: Similarly, Islam does not permit sexually exciting dancing or any other erotic activity, such as suggestive or obscene songs, provocative dramas, and every type of rubbish which some people today term "art" and "progress."

This is the secret behind the significant words of the Quran prohibiting fornication and adultery (both of which are known as zina in Arabic).

> **And do not come near zina; indeed, it is an abomination and an evil way.** (17:32)

<u>Making Statues and Similar Articles</u>: Islam prohibits the acquisition of statues and even more strongly the making of them.

<u>Drawings, Paintings, or Photography</u>: They are either permitted or disapproved, "depending on what comes closest to the spirit of the Islamic Legislation…Their subject matter should not be sexually provocative, as, for example, the erotic parts of the female body or a man and woman in a state of intimacy, and should not be of someone sacred or respected, such as the angels or the prophets."

<u>Manufacturing Intoxicants and Drugs</u>: Islam prohibits any participation in the promotion of alcoholic beverages, whether it be in their manufacture, distribution, or consumption…The case of other intoxicants and drugs, such as hashish, cocaine, and the like, is the same.[11]

<u>Prohibited Kinds of Trade</u>: Islam only prohibits trade that is unjust, either through exorbitant profit or promotes something that is unlawful. "It is haram to do business in alcoholic beverages, intoxicants, drugs, swine, idols, statues or anything of this sort whose consumption and use Islam has prohibited."

The merchant should beware of cheating, for the cheater is outside the community of Islam; he should beware of tampering with the scales when weighing; beware of hoarding lest he forfeit the protection of Allah and His Messenger (peace be upon him); and beware of dealing in usury or interest (riba), for Allah has prohibited it…[12]

<u>Prohibited Types of Employment</u>: Jobs which are detrimental to the cause of Islam, or which harms Muslims, or any other service which supports an unjust action or promotes what is haram is itself haram. However, "**under the compulsion of unavoidable necessity, the Muslim may seek temporary employment in such**

activities to the extent of what is required, but he should in the meantime be searching for other gainful employments until Allah opens a way for him, for indeed Allah does open the door for those who sincerely seek to avoid what is haram.[13]

'At least' for 'the favor of' making Quraysh Habitually secure—secure in their trading Caravan 'to Yemen' in the winter and Syria in the summer—let them worship the Lord of this 'Sacred' house—Who has fed them against hunger and made them secure Against fear.[14]

ENDNOTES

[1] Ali, Abdullah Yusuf, The Holy Quran, Page 284, Goodword Books, 2007
[2] Qaradawi, Yusuf al, The Lawful and Prohibited In Islam, Page 127, Dar Al Taqwa LTD, 2011
[3] Ibid. Page 145
[4] Ibid. Pages 128-129
[5] Ibid. Page 131
[6] Ibid. Page 132
[7] Ibid. Page 137
[8] Ibid. Page 143
[9] Ibid. Page 134
[10] Ibid. Page 130
[11] Ibid. Pages 134-136
[12] Ibid. Pages 141-142
[13] Ibid. Page 145
[14] Khattab, Mustafa, The Clear Quran, Page 284, Book of Signs Foundation, 2016

Chapter 11

CRIME AND CRIMINOLOGY

A theory of Emile Durkheim explained criminality as a function of social strain produced when peoples' expectations do not match their level of legitimate access to material wealth and social status. This being the case, it is understandable that impoverished and isolated groups who have fewer legitimate options, a life of crime is often considered a reasonable alternative.[1]

BLACK AND WHITE PARALLEL UNIVERSES

After World War II, the feeling that accompanied victory and the energy of post WWII prosperity, produced the belief that American ingenuity could solve all of (white) America's problems. The new concept of urban renewal had resulted from the 1939 World's Fair. In Flushing Meadows Corona Park, Queens, 62 miles of roads, 200 buildings housed the works of 1,354 exhibitors from 58 nations and 33 states. But the problems of America's black universe began in 1619 and for the most part still exist today.

Ferguson, Missouri initially was an all white city which was guarded by both customs and laws, even after racially zoning laws were made illegal in 1917. There were legal loopholes that allowed private contracts to continue the practice of racial zoning (unofficially of course). St. Louis was also a city that practiced racially segregated zoning even after the Great Migration of blacks moving to the north after WWI. White northerners fought to abolish slavery during the Civil War, but that did not mean they wanted to have black neighbors. This black migration eventually produced the new phenomenon of "White flight." Because in 1948, "a case involving the sale of a house roughly eight miles from Ferguson in which the Supreme Court took down restrictive racial covenants."

To the surprise of almost no one, the high court's determination coincided with the sentiments that brought about "White flight," or the movement of White families (and necessary resources) out of the cities and into the suburbs. This trend largely animated the decline of urban America in the second half of the twentieth century. Over the next twenty years, nearly 60 percent of the White population of St. Louis left the city.[2]

You can not have a city without people so the St. Louis' Comprehensive City Plan of 1947 was produced. The unsightliness of city slums became an issue. Not out of concern for the people who lived in the slums but for those who had to see them during their daily commutes to and from work or when visiting the downtown areas for entertainment. The new public housing development project became known as "the projects". This cleared the city of both white slums and black slums and replaced them in a way that maintained the desired racial segregation. The most famous of the new St. Louis projects was the Pruitt-Igoe developments, named for Wendell O. Pruitt, an African-American pilot who was one of the Tuskegee Airmen who fought in World War II. "A multi structure complex containing 2,870 housing units on 56 acres...Built on the remains of the African-American neighborhood of Desoto-Carr, which had once been home to 3200 families, it was designed to house Black residents in the Pruitt homes." Public housing was to be sited downtown - "certainly nowhere near the prosperous suburbs – and at high density, so as to leave the commercial core of the city intact."

Yet, ironically, all along subsidies in the form of Federal Housing Administration (FHA) loans–"giveaways" of a different sort–were assisting White homeowners as they moved to the suburbs, to sites from which Blacks were by definition excluded. The agency even forbade loans to female-headed households and pledged to avoid loan practices that might force together "inharmonious racial or nationality groups."[3]

One could say that public housing was designed to fail because its motivation was not human compassion, but instead a penitentiary mentality. The goal was to hide the city's struggling peoples, and to punish them for being poor and standing in the way of progress. Approximately thirty years later the Pruitt-Igoe projects were leveled and its land returned to nature. "And where did the people who lived at Pruitt-Igoe and in other projects go? They moved to Ferguson."

Had Michael Brown survived his assault by Officer Darren

Wilson, or if the incident between Brown and Wilson had never even happened, inevitably, Brown would have had another encounter with the criminal justice system. By his early twenties and almost certainly by his late twenties, Michael Brown would have been accused of, confessed to, or been found guilty of a crime, whether he committed the crime or not. He would have gone where so many members of America's "disposable" populations ultimately go: prison…The racial disparities here are quite stark. African-Americans make up roughly 13 percent of the American population but 36 percent of the 2.2 million Americans incarcerated today.[4]

The loophole in the thirteenth Amendment (the abolishment of slavery except as a punishment of a crime) allowed the continuation of slavery in a different form. First the vagrancy laws were included in the Black Codes of the post Civil War era. This "helped reinforce the notion of exclusion by criminalizing homelessness, unemployment, and arbitrarily conceived offenses like 'using insulting language in the presence of a female". It almost amounted to a black person might go to prison just for committing the crime of being black. With the Enlightenment came the idea that prisons should be a more humane approach to punishment. One of the results was that the Biblical approach should be used where prisons were replaced by reformatories and hard work, isolation and the reading of the Bible would enable the criminal to return to society as a law abiding citizen. The first two American prisons that tried to implement a version of this new method of rehabilitation were the Eastern State Penitentiary in Philadelphia and the Auburn Prison in Up-state New York. The following is the conclusion that Charles Dickens came to after visiting the Eastern State Penitentiary:

> His visit, which he chronicled in the splenetic and tendentious American Notes for General Circulation, disappointed him. Dickens was offended by Americans' course manners (especially by the practice of chewing and spitting tobacco), nauseated by the moral transgressions of slavery, turned off by Americans' gross materialism, and deeply unsettled by the nation's hypocrisy. America was "not the republic I came to see," he wrote a friend, "…not the republic of my imagination." He had found, in America, "old vices in new forms.[5]

Michael Ignatieff explained in his very impactful prison history study on the changing roles of prisons, "For the pains of neglect." Ignatieff and other scholars, the philosopher Michael Foucault, the sociologist Erving Gofman, and historian David J. Rothman all sparked the reconsideration of American prison history and ideology during the mid to late twentieth century. They all agreed that the proper understanding of a penal institution was to see it less as an institution of reform and more as an institution of total control where the inmates would be like mice in a laboratory. However, the object of experimentation would not be limited to criminals, but should also include the poor, insane and criminals, all lumped together in a project under the title of "Asylum". But one should not assume the term "asylum" has any connection to protection and shelter, the real role that it was intended to play was "the coercion of human personality and consciousness, the eradication of differences, and the practices of social control." Foucault pointed out that the true goal, hidden behind a sympathetic mask, was political and disciplinary. Prisons for the lower class criminals, and should include other equally controlling social institutions like schools, factories, mental institutions, and the military, with the intention of producing "docile bodies" that would be incapable of challenging the ruling elite.[6]

Thanks to the well documented trend that has positioned America as the world's leading incarcerator-nation, one in every twenty-eight American children has a parent in prison. Nearly half of these children—46 percent, to be precise—are Black. It is no surprise that in 2013, the popular PBS children's show Sesame Street deemed it appropriate to include a new muppet character, Alex, whose chief identifying characteristic is that his father is serving time.[7]

MAY ALLAH HELP US

ENDNOTES

[1] Abdul-Salaam, Sabur, Rise and Fall of Great Empires – Black Lives Matter, Page 85, Sabur Abdul-Salaam, 2021
[2] Hill, Marc Lamont, Nobody, Page 7, Simon and Schuster Inc., 2016
[3] Ibid. Page 17
[4] Ibid. Page 123
[5] Ibid. Page 130
[6] Ibid. Pages 131-132
[7] Ibid. Pages 124-125

Chapter 12

DIVINE, NATURAL AND HUMAN POWER

Oh Allah! Lord of Power (and Rule), You give Power to whom You please, and you strip off Power from whom You please: You endue with Honor whom You please, and You bring low Whom You please: in Your hand is all Good. Surely, over all things You have Power. [1]

Allah is the source of all power and every action happens with the permission of Allah. Allah could just have a desire and that desire would come into existence ("be" and it is). However, Allah does not have to give individual commands to make all of His desires happen, He uses systems (or laws) to implement many of His desires. He does not have to give an individual command to make each apple fall from an apple tree. Allah created the "law of gravity," movement downward resulting from gravitational attraction. Nor does Allah have to command each human being to take each breath, breathing is part of the respiratory system. So Allah is the source of all power but I call the power that exists in the universe "natural power" (wind, rain, fire etc.):

He is the One Who sends the winds ushering in His mercy. When they bear heavy clouds, We drive them to a lifeless land and then cause rain to fall, producing every type of fruit. [2]

Have you considered the fire you kindle? Is it you who produce its trees, or is it We Who do so? [3]

And We send the fecundating winds, then cause rain to descend from the sky, therewith providing you with water (in abundance), though you are not the guardians of its stores. [4]

Among His signs are this, that He sends the Winds, as heralds of Glad Tidings, giving you a taste of His (Grace and) Mercy–that the ships may sail (majestically) by His Command and that you may seek of His Bounty: in order that you may be grateful. [5]

Natural Power is consistent. The earth has been revolving around the sun for millions of years and we can still predict (insha Allah/ God willing) the time the sun will rise and set each day.

However, what I call "human power", humans' ability using sight, hearing, touch etc., to transfer information to the brain, and the brains' ability to process that information and use it to create new inventions that have radically changed life on earth, but "human power" is not consistent. New inventions can sometimes change life for the better but it often causes more harm than good.

We have indeed created man in the best of molds, then we abase him (to be) the lowest of the low – Except such as believe and do righteous deeds. [6]

The Quran tells us that every soul has acknowledged that Allah is their Lord (7:172), but only religious faith will enable them to continue its acknowledgment. However, because of man's natural curiosity, he will see the sun rise and set each day and humans who don't believe in a Supreme Being, may attribute it to some natural laws (or Mother Nature), that govern the universe. There are obstacles that prevent some people from having the correct understanding of "natural power." The main obstacle is ignorance of Divine knowledge. Almost everyone acknowledges the importance of the acquisition of knowledge, but the acquisition of knowledge should be accompanied with a good intention, because knowledge can be a blessing or a curse.

In Jeffery Sachs' book The Ages of Globalization, he divides history into seven ages of globalization, the following are the first six. The Paleolithic Age (70,000 -10,000 BCE). The Neolithic Age (10,000 - 3,000 BCE). The Equestrian Age (3,000 - 1,000 BCE). The

Classical Age (1,000 BCE - 1500 CE). The Ocean Age (1500 - 1800 CE). The Industrial Age (1800 - 2000 CE). So when Adam and Eve were sent down to earth, no longer being in the garden meant they had to work to provide for their family. According to Sachs, based on archaeological and anthropological evidence, hunters and gatherers seemed to have had better nutrition, fewer diseases, less strenuous labor and longer lives than their contemporary farm households. However, in spite of the advantages of the nomadic life, in the end, settled agriculture was the winner.

> Yet the outcome may have been a lowering of average wellbeing in the process, perhaps the one described by the biblical "expulsion from Eden," in which a life of leisurely foraging in the garden was replaced by a life of arduous farm labor. God's punishment to Adam and Eve for eating the fruit of the tree of knowledge is stated: "By the sweat of your brow you shall eat bread, Until you return to the ground, from which you were taken."[7]

> For thousands of years, up to the start of industrialization itself, almost all of humanity lived in rural areas. It was the natural power of the sun and wind that were crucial for agriculture which eventually facilitated the Neolithic Revolution which gave rise to villages and eventually cities.[8]

> In Sachs' chapter The Ocean Age, the section The New European Age of Inquiry, he points out that the fall of Constantinople and the discovery of the sea routes to America and Asia did bring about new global trade routes but also had a tremendous impact on the European mind. "The discovery of new lands based on new technologies radically altered the European worldview." Other contributing factors were empiricism and science in general.[9]

Even though Sachs did mention the Muslims' contribution in another section, I wonder why it was not mentioned in The New European Age of Inquiry?

> Today's Islamic world is fragmented, yet the Golden Age of Islam under the Abbasid Caliphate of Baghdad reminds us of the era when Islamic scholars led the world in knowledge and sought ancient wisdom from all sources in order to create an integrated knowledge and science. That noble effort saved

much of the Classical heritage for later generations, including our own.[10]

If one wonders why the New European Age of Inquiry did not appear until the 15th century, one could also come to the conclusion that ignorance/arrogance and greed will always be obstacles in the pursuit of truth and progress. Early Christian scholars' belief that the sun was fixed and the earth orbited around the sun and rotated on an axis, prevented them from advancing in the area of astronomy. The Islamic belief that Allah (God) is the all Powerful, all Knowing Creator of the Universe, and that the earth is just a small part of His creation, removed that obstacle.[11]

Where ignorance often slows down mankind's achievements, greed is always destructive and often causes the corruption of "human power"

INSATIABLE GREED OF THE EMPIRE BUILDERS

It was one thing to exploit the native populations and grab their lands; it was another to create an ethos that justified such actions. The Christian virtues of temperance and charity had long preached self-control over the passions for wealth and glory. A new morality was needed to justify the remarkable efforts toward conquest and the subjugation of whole populations. Over time, the justification was the idea that conquest was a God-given right, even a responsibility, to bring civilization to the heathens.[12]

The United States is the richest country in the world with the most billionaires, in spite of the fact that it is just a baby compared to other nations and empires. Egypt (6,000 BC), India (1700 BC), Greece (1100 BC), Iran (Persia 238 BC), Italy (Rome 800 BC), Germany (Steppe People 400 BC), India (Mauryan 500 BC), China (Han Empire 221 BC), Japan (Yayoi period 300 BC) and the United States (1776 CE).[13]

Obviously America's size and natural resources (the land taken from the Native Americans) is one of the main contributing factors for America's economic growth.

As well as over 200 years of free African slave labor. But in my opinion, it was not those two factors that enabled America to have the number of billionaires that they now have. Other countries colonized and exploited lands and people but still do not have the number of billionaires that America has. America's wealth and wealth inequality is partly due to the American value of individualism, but not just the value of individualism alone, it is America's culture and social structure that sets America apart from other countries. To get a better understanding of American individualism, you need to look at America's culture and social structure but first we have to look at the role a society's culture and social structure is supposed to play in general.

"Culture provides individuals with a set of common understandings that they use to fashion their actions. It allows us to 'know' in rather broad terms what we can expect of others and what they can expect of us". Culture allows people to know the dos and the don'ts, mental stop and go signs that help us to navigate our everyday lives. "In providing common understandings, culture binds the separated lives of individuals into a large whole, making society possible by providing a common framework of meaning".

Now let us look a little closer at norms, values and language, three key components of culture. Norms help people to know what actions are permissible and what actions are not. It is okay when given permission to borrow your neighbor's lawn mower, but it is not okay to steal it. So norms are social rules that define acceptable and unacceptable behaviors in different situations. These social rules are especially important in the areas of sex, property and safety.[14]

Values differ from norms in that norms are rules concerning behavior, "values are broad ideas regarding what is desirable, correct and good that most members of a society share". As I mentioned before, "individuality" has always been a very important value within American culture. Other important values are "achievement and success, work and activity, efficiency and practicallity, material comfort...progress, rationality, patriotism and democracy (Williams 1970). Values are important contributing factors in the life choices that people make.

"Language is the cornerstone of every culture. It is the chief vehicle by which people communicate ideas, information, attitudes and emotions to one another, and it is the principle means by which human beings create culture and transmit it from generation to generation."[15]

Social Structure - "The interweaving of people's interactions and relationships in more or less recurrent and stable patterns." We can say culture deals with the customs a people have by providing a framework that allows people to interpret events and guides their actions. Social structure through recurring and orderly relationships, gives us the feeling of comfort and security that comes with living an organized and stable life. However, sociologists have found by studying race, class and gender, the feeling of comfort and security is not always enjoyed by all members of society. "From this perspective, race, class and gender are forms of inequality that profoundly affect human experience and operate as interlocking systems of priviledge and oppression."[16]

Both the name and the concept of democracy originated in ancient Greece. It meant "rule of the people." In the Greek city-states, particularly Athens, slaves and women were excluded from the vote so only a minority of the inhabitants (20-30%) were active citizens.[17]

Culture being the bond that binds the lives of individuals into the large whole, with a common meaningful framework, which enables the creation of a society. Then a common language acts as the cornerstone of the culture by enabling people to communicate ideas, information and emotions to one another. The league of the Iroquois, the most powerful of America's northeastern tribes, consisted of thousands of people bound together by a common Iroquois language and destiny.

In the vision of the Mohawk chief Hiawatha, the legendary Dekaniwidah spoke to the Iroquois: "We bind ourselves together by taking hold of each other's hands so firmly and forming a circle so strong that if a tree should fall upon it, it could not shake or break it, so that our people and grandchildren shall remain in the circle in security, peace and happiness.[18]

When a culture has been ingrained in a people for hundreds of years, a bond of love and respect is produced that is almost unbreakable. The Italians, Germans and other immigrants probably enjoyed similar cultural bonds from their respective countries before landing on the shores of the Americas'. But after arriving in the Americas, the cultural bonds based on love and respect were replaced with the American cultural value of "individuality."

THE AMERICAN MOSAIC

The peopling of America is one of the great dramas in all of human history. Over the years, a massive stream of humanity...crossed every ocean and continent to reach the United States. They came speaking every language and representing every nationality, race and religion. Today, there are more people of Irish ancestry in the United States than in Ireland, more Jews than in Israel, and more blacks than in most African countries.[19]

Ethnocentrism is the point of view "in which one's own group is the center of everything, and all others are scaled and rated with reference to it." This point of view is a result of a society's culture has become so deeply ingrained that they become second nature, making it very difficult to conceive or understand other ways of life. The feeling that our group is the best group (tribe, nation, religion, political party etc.) is a social glue that binds people together, but it can also create intergroup conflicts.[20]

Institutions are the social structures that are created to organize, direct and execute the essential tasks of life. They are usually built upon a standard solution to a set of problems. America's founding fathers, in order to maintain slavery or cheap labor, established the concept of white supremacy through "institutional racism."

This pre-existing predisposition towards whiteness would reinforce the parallel impetus found among virtually every immigrant group that has come to America, namely the will to join American whiteness. Indeed, so powerful has this enticement been that the initial exclusion of Jews, Slavs, Armenians, Syrians, Irishmen and others would only result in a redoubling of efforts to gain admission rather than oppose white supremacy on substantive or moral grounds...As Richard Dyer notes in his book WHITE, "Because whiteness carries such rewards and privileges, the sense of a border that might be crossed and a hierarchy that might be climbed has produced a dynamic that has enthralled people who have had any chance of participating in it.[21]

RACISM, CAPITALISM, AND BILLIONAIRES

From the time of America's founding fathers, there have been two parallel universes, a white universe and a black universe. Howard Zinn includes the following quote in his book People's History of the United States.

> African slavery is hardly to be praised. But it was far different from plantation or mining slavery in the Americas, which was lifelong, morally crippling, destructive of family ties, without hope of any future. African slavery lacked two elements that made American slavery the most cruel form of slavery in History: the frenzy for limitless profit that comes from capitalistic agriculture; the reduction of the slave to less than human status by the use of racial hatred, with that relentless clarity based on color, where white was master, black was slave.[22]

Most billionaires are evil people. I realize that billionaires are a Twentieth Century Phenomenon, but my phrase could be replaced with, "most of the top 1% are evil people." Meaning they do not usually get that rich by being nice guys and they have been able to do it through a legal (but often unethical) political and economic framework. Most low wage workers are employed by large corporations. By Walmart giving their workers low salaries and minimal benefits, by 2012 they were able to pay their CEO an annual salary of $20.7 million.

> Not incidentally, the wealth of the Walton family—which still owns the lion's share of the Walmart stock—by then exceeded the wealth of the bottom 40 percent of American families combined, according to an analysis by the Economic Policy Institute.[23]

The United States is a unique society. By it being a society consisting almost entirely of immigrants and the descendants of immigrants, American culture does not bind the separate lives of individuals into a large whole the same way many other cultures do. Some countries take pride in the social services they provide for their citizens. And some countries take pride in the elementary and secondary education they provide for their children. While others may take pride in the quality of their infrastructure. These services cost money which necessitates the raising of taxes but also produces good paying jobs. Hence, those countries have fewer billionaires and less wealth inequality. America takes pride in its gross national product (GDP). America's most important value is individualism, not rationality, patriotism or democracy, and this has corrupted America's "human power".

The splitting of the atom has made it possible for inventions that have improved the lives of countless numbers of people, while at the same time it is responsible for the production of weapons of mass destruction. The sun provides us with solar power and is making our lives better, while fossil fuels have greatly contributed to global warming which may eventually bring about the earth's destruction. Allah has given humans a brain and has made us His representative on earth. It was our responsibility to use the natural resources that we have been blessed with in ways that would benefit humans, animals and the earth itself. But unfortunately we the Muslims have not provided the spiritual guidance that is necessary to take people out of the darkness and into the light. However, we will in the future because eventually, the Believers will be successful.

ALLAHU AKBAR

ENDNOTES

[1] Ali, Abdullah Yusuf, The Holy Quran, Pages 33 & 34, Goodword Books, 2007
[2] Khattab, Mustafa, The Clear Quran, Page 84, Book of Signs Foundation, 2016
[3] Ibid. Page 313
[4] Ali, Abdullah Yusuf, The Holy Quran, Page 175, Goodword Books, 2007
[5] Ibid. Page 284
[6] Ibid. Page 434
[7] Sachs, Jeffrey D., The Ages of Globalization, Page 43, Columbia University Press, 2020
[8] Ibid. Page 5
[9] Ibid. Page 104
[10] Ibid. Page 94
[11] Philips, Abu Ameenah Bilal, The Clash of Civilizations (An Islamic View), Page 18, Al-Hidaayah Publishing and Distribution LTD, 2007
[12] Sachs, Jeffrey D., The Ages of Globalization, Page 114, Columbia University Press, 2020
[13] Woolf, Alex, A Short History of the World, Page 5, Metro Books, 2008
[14] Hughes, Michael and Kroehler, Carolyn J. and VanderZAnden, James W., Sociology the Core, Pages 42 & 43, McGraw-Hill, 2002
[15] Ibid. Pages 45 & 46
[16] Ibid. Pages 54-56
[17] Philips, Abu Ameenah Bilal, The Clash of Civilizations (An Islamic View), Page 25, Al-Hidaayah Publishing and Distribution LTD, 2007
[18] Abdul-Salaam, Sabur, Rise and Fall of Great Empires – Black Lives Matter, Page 17, Sabur Abdul-Salaam, 2021
[19] Sowell, Thomas, Ethnic America, Page 3, Basic Books, Inc., 1981
[20] Hughes, Michael and Kroehler, Carolyn J. and Vander Zanden, James W., Sociology the Core, Page 49, McGraw Hill 2002
[21] Jackson, Sherman A., Islam and the Black American, Pages 80 & 81, New York, Oxford University Press, 2005
[22] Abdul-Salaam, Sabur, Rise and Fall of Great Empires – Black Lives Matter, Pages 81 & 82, Sabur Abdul-Salaam, 2021
[23] Ibid. Pages 97-100

EPILOGUE

During the covid19 lockdown I began watching Friday khutbahs on Youtube and I continued this practice even after I resumed attending Salat-al-Jumah prayers in the masjid. There are around a half a dozen Imams whose khutbahs I usually watch/listen to on Youtube regularly. Today I chose to watch a khutbah on suicides in America because it dealt with a very serious current problem that doesn't usually get the attention it deserves in the Muslim community. Me being a student of history and modern Western culture, I was aware of the seriousness of the problem but most of the adult Muslims are not. Both the Imam who was giving the khutbah and I agreed on the seriousness of the problem, but we disagreed on the cause and solution. The Imam explained how a young Muslim brother told him he had wanted to commit suicide but his love for his mother and not wanting to cause her any pain stopped him from doing it. The young brother's love for his mother was a blessing but it was not a good reason for him to not commit suicide. What about displeasing Allah or spending eternity in the Hellfire? Will he commit suicide if his mother dies?

The Imam pointed out that many Muslims are experiencing depression and it is important that they should get professional help and I think that is very good advice. The Imam also said that it is very important that our children know we love them, but I think that it is more important that they know that Allah loves them. The young Imam's parents were from a Muslim country but the Imam was born and raised in the United States, he was very intelligent and had graduate degrees from a prestigious university in a Muslim country, however the suicide problem is a relatively recent problem for the American middle-class, but the minorities and the poor have been struggling with suicide for centuries (alcoholism and drug abuse are just slow forms of suicide). I may not have agreed with everything that the Imam said but I know that his intention was good. However, Umar, may Allah be pleased with him said:

I am afraid, he who has been brought up in Islam and has no knowledge of jahiliyyah [un-Islamic culture and philosophy], may become an instrument disintegrating Islam unknowingly.

My older brother and I never lived with our father and we grew up in a proud but poor family. My brother died from an overdose of heroin a week before his 25th birthday, and I at one time used to use all kinds of drugs but Allah blessed me to hate needles. I didn't even like doctors or nurses giving me needles so there was no way that I was going to put a needle in my own arm. But that hatred of needles was a blessing from Allah and one of the proofs that Allah loved me.

In Mustapha Sheikh's book A Treasury of Ibn Taymiyyah (His Timeless Thought and Wisdom), in the section entitled "Real Love", the story of Moses and the shepherd is told:

In this story, Moses comes by a shepherd on his knees with his hands spread out to the sky, praying. Although delighted at first, Moses soon hears the shepherd's prayer: 'Oh, my beloved God, I love You more than You can know. I will do anything for you, just say the word. Even if You asked me to slaughter the fattest sheep in my flock in Your name, I would do so without hesitation. You would roast it and put its tail fat in Your rice to make it more tasty. Afterward I would wash Your feet and clean Your ears and pick Your lice for You. That is how much I love you.' Besides himself in anger, Moses interrupts the shepherd and accuses him of sheer blasphemy. Ashamed by what he has done, the shepherd apologizes repeatedly and promises to pray as decent people do. Later Moses hears God's voice: 'Oh Moses, what have you done? You scolded that poor shepherd and failed to realize how dear he is to Me. He might not be saying the right things in the right way, but he is sincere. His heart is pure and his intentions good. I am pleased with him. His words might be blasphemy to your ears, but to Me they are sweet blasphemy.'

In his own way, Shaykh-al-Islam also wants to bring to the fore the importance of protecting the belief of the masses, in this case by defending a doctrine of love against the interventions of a scholarly elite who preach to the rest that the term love, when used in the Qur'an and Sunnah, is but a metaphor for God's will. Against this, Ibn Taymiyyah argues not just for the possibility, and even necessity, of affirming that God loves—he argues that God's love is one aspect of the fundamental bond between the Creator and creation.

The reason many young Muslims in the United States (and many of us old Muslims also) have mental and emotional problems, in many cases, is our knowledge and practice of Islam is inadequate. Because of that problem the Quran and Allah's Deen is unable to heal our hearts and the heart is the most important piece of flesh in the body. We the parents have done our children a disservice by prioritizing the primary, secondary and academic institutions of higher education while neglecting their Islamic growth and development. Going to the masjid's Sunday school one day a week was not enough and we could not supplement their Islamic deficiencies because we could not give them something we did not have. Our words may have said "love Allah", but our actions said, "love the dunya." So yes, Muslim children should love their parents but it should always be made clear to them that love of Allah has to come first. If a Muslim's desire to please Allah is not enough to convince him or her not to commit suicide, then surely fear of the Hellfire will be, insha-Allah.

Huthayfa ibn al Yamaan (May Allah be pleased with him) reported:

"The people used to ask the Messenger of Allah (Peace and blessings of Allah be upon him) about the good, and I used to ask about evil out of fear of it reaching me. I asked, 'O Messenger of Allah (pbuh), we were living in ignorance and evil, then Allah brought this good to us. Will there be any evil after this good?' He replied, 'Yes.' Then I asked, 'Will there be any good after that evil?' He replied, 'yes, but it will be tainted.' So, I asked, 'What will be its taint?' He replied, 'A people who guide others to other than my Sunnah (way). You will approve of some of their deeds and disapprove of others.' I further asked, 'Then will there be any evil after that good?' He said, 'Yes, callers at the gates of Hell. Whoever responds to their call, they will throw him into the Fire.' I then said, 'O Messenger of Allah, describe them to us.' He said, 'They will be from our people and speak our language.' I asked, 'So what do you order me to do if that reaches me?' He said, 'Stick to the united body of Muslims and their leader (Imam).' I further asked, 'What if they have neither a united body nor a leader?' He replied, 'Then keep away from all of those sects, even if you have to bite on the roots of a tree until death reaches you and you are in that state." (Muslim)

Sheikh Abdullah Hakim Quick (Ph.D.) says in his commentary on this hadith the following:

Taqwa and knowledge should not be based on clothing, race, genealogy or language. Sometimes the longest beard or the biggest cap or the best face covering only hide hypocrisy and arrogance. In this Hadith, the Prophet (pbuh) gives us

a piercing look into the future where even people, Islamic in appearance, or people gifted with the Arabic language, could be leading humanity straight to hell.

BIBLIOGRAPHY

Abdul-Salaam, Sabur, Rise and Fall of Great Empires – Black Lives Matter, Sabur Abdul-Salaam, 2021

Abdul-Salaam, Sabur, Spiritual Journey of an American Muslim, Sabur Abdul-Salaam, 2013

Abdul-Salaam, Sabur, Who Speaks For the Muslims In America, Sabur Abdul-Salaam, 2016

Ahmed, Hasanuddin, A Brief History of Islam, Goodword Books, 2010

Al-Ghazali, Muhammad, A Thematic Commentary on the Quran, The International Institute of Islamic Thought, 2000

Ali, Abdullah Yusuf, The Holy Quran, Goodword Books, 2007

Hedges, Chris, America: The Farewell Tour, Simon & Schuster, 2018

Hill, Marc Lamont, Nobody, Simon & Schuster Inc., 2016

Hughes, Michael and Kroehler, Carolyn J. and Vander Zanden, James W., Sociology the Core, McGraw - Hill, 2002

Jackson, Sherman A., Islam and the Black American, New York, Oxford University Press, 2005

Janssen, Sarah (Senior Editor), The World Almanac, Infobase, 2020

Khattab, Mustafa, The Clear Quran, Book of Signs Foundation, 2016

Mawdudi, Sayyid Abul A'la, Towards Understanding the Quran, The Islamic Foundation, 2006

Michalak-Pikulska, Barbara and Piela, Marek and Majtezak, Tomas Z., Oriental Languages and Civilizations, Jagielionian University Press, Krakow, 2020

Nadwi, Sayyed Abul Hasan Ali., Islam and the World, UK Islamic Academy, 2005

Openstax, Introduction to Sociology 2 E, Rice University, 2016

Philips, Abu Ameenah Bilal, The Clash of Civilizations (An Islamic View), Al-Hidaayah Publishing and Distribution LTD, 2007

Qaradawi, Yusuf al, The Lawful and Prohibited In Islam, Dar Al Taqwa LTD, 2011

Robinson, Jackie, Negroe Leagues and major leagues prospects, Wikipedia, 1995

Sachs, Jeffrey D., The Ages of Globalization, Columbia University Press, 2020

Sieny, Mahmoud Esma'il, Heroes of Islam, Darussalam Publishing House, 2000

Sowell, Thomas, Ethnic America, Basic Books Inc., 1981

Sullivan, Dylan and Hickel, Jason, How British Colonialism Killed 100 Million Indians in 40 Years, ALJAZEERA, 2 December 2022

Woolf, Alex, A Short History of the World, Metro Books, 2008

Made in the USA
Columbia, SC
10 August 2024

d9b240cf-3446-4653-95f1-440ac175e1d6R03